7/19/44

Birthday
        Greetings!

                Harriet Agler

MARTIN NIEMOELLER
Hero of the Concentration Camp

MARTIN NIEMOELLER

Hero of the Concentration Camp

BASIL MILLER

(Second Edition)

ZONDERVAN PUBLISHING HOUSE
Grand Rapids, Michigan

EIGHT FORTY-SEVEN OTTAWA AVENUE
GRAND RAPIDS, MICHIGAN

ACKNOWLEDGMENT

THE task of writing the life of Martin Niemoeller under existing conditions must be recognized as difficult indeed. The famous German pastor is in a concentration camp, and all contact with sources in Germany, such as the files of newspapers, magazines, court documents, due to the war, is severed. More irreparable, however, is the loss of contact with the Niemoeller family and close friends, who would be able to furnish material not otherwise available about the pastor.

In doing the research for this biography I have covered diligently all published materials concerning Niemoeller available in the United States. Since much of this information is duplicated in various sources the task of making acknowledgment to them all is unnecessary and useless. However, I must acknowledge my debt to the following who have been most helpful:

The Library of Congress for Martin Niemoeller's *Vom U-Boot zur Kanzel,* which is the German source for Niemoeller's U-boat experiences.

The German author, writing anonymously, of *Martin Niemoeller und sein Bekenntnis,* which is published in Switzerland, and which appeared in England under the title, *Pastor Niemoeller and His Creed.* Dr. Hans Weigert, now serving as professor at Trinity College, Hartford, Conn., and a former member of Niemoeller's Berlin church, believes this work to have been written by Pastor Hildebrand. Also my debt must be acknowledged to Dr. Weigert for his aid in the research.

ACKNOWLEDGMENT

Willett, Clark and Company for permission to quote from *From U-Boat to Pulpit,* and Niemoeller's sermons, entitled, *Here Stand I;* as well as to Niemoeller's other book of sermons published in America under the title of *God Is My Fuehrer.* In these messages one feels the pulsations of Niemoeller's own heartbeats.

Dr. Henry Smith Leiper, American Secretary of the World Council of Churches, for permission to use and quote the various articles which have appeared under his name in the American press, as well as his addition to the American edition of Niemoeller's *From U-Boat to Pulpit.*

Dr. Ewart E. Turner, who for four years was pastor of the American Church in Berlin. I am especially indebted to Dr. Turner for recent information concerning the Niemoeller family, the pastor's father and mother.

Dr. Paul Hutchinson, for permission to quote from his article on Niemoeller in the *Atlantic Monthly.*

The Christian Century, The Christian Advocate and *The Catholic World,* for permission to quote from and use articles published by them. American and English newspapers and reports have furnished an unexcelled aid for direct information concerning the day-by-day, running story of the pastor's contact with Hitler before and after his arrest.

Dr. Alex Krag, California linguist, and former professor of German at Asbury College and Pasadena College, has rendered great assistance in checking German translations, for which I am grateful. Nor can I forget the aid my wife, Esther Miller, has been in checking source materials, doing research

ACKNOWLEDGMENT

and confirming quotations. Librarians have been hounded and file rooms haunted in this search for the true story of this man who dares defy Hitler, and to all who have thus assisted I say, "Thank you," especially to the Huntington Library and the Pasadena Public Library for making source materials available.

BASIL MILLER

Pasadena, California.

CONTENTS

Chapter I

HERO IN THE MAKING

HERE is a man, this Martin Niemoeller, in whose soul there is no "Heil Hitler!"

He is God's man of destiny for modern Germany's hour of tragedy. God has matched spiritual need with a man whose life has been steel-fibered. He has gone through Hitler's crucible of suffering and persecution, sufficient to tangle the sky-high purposes of lesser God-minded men, only to come out dominant in faith and holding aloft the battle flag of religious freedom.

He owes allegiance to no iron-heeled tyrant, bowing in obeisance only to the Master by whose Spirit he has been conquered.

Hitler's panzer divisions might sweep with a victorious tread through Europe—crumbling thrones, tottering empires, laying waste nations; but before the triumphant spirit of Martin Niemoeller they fall back defeated—the iron of their machinery powerless against the steel of his soul.

Hitler's luftwaffe might blast to rock-heaps once proud Warsaw; but Martin Niemoeller, founded upon the Rock, defies their winged deviltry. Hitler's armies may capture France's Maginot Line, thereby shackling with slavery's chains a nation's body and soul; but there is a line of Christian defense around Martin Niemoeller, from which the Hand that guides the wheels of time commands, "Thus far and no farther."

9

Hitler's flying fortresses might bomb England's hoary-haired cathedrals, Holland's ivied shrines; but this ruthless dictator's mastermind has devised no demolition instrument sufficiently powerful to loosen one tiny stone from the Altar at which Martin Niemoeller bows in worship.

Hitler's quislings might throw Denmark into the hungry maw of this conquest-crazed dictator, sell Sweden for the price of human skulls; but there have been no traitors in his new German religion wise enough, diabolical enough, to alter Martin Niemoeller's allegiance to "the old Book and the old Faith."

Hitler might stain the sword of his dictatorship with the blood of a million Jews, a million patriotic Czechs, purged Hollanders, fighting Greeks; but the sight of this red-running sword throws no terror into Niemoeller's washed-white soul.

Hitler might rewrite the creed until he and not God stands first therein, reshape religion into the mold of his new Germanic, Aryan cast; but he cannot rewrite one line of the Bible, restate one tenet of Martin Luther's credo for Niemoeller.

For Martin Niemoeller there is no new social order Hitler-hued; no master Aryan race; no super nation binding into a Hitler-whole the lesser races and peoples of the earth. The Kingdom of God to this Martin is the superstructure in which races and kindreds, blood and ancestry, Jew and Gentile alike, become one through Christ-redemption.

He dared cry out, "God is my Fuehrer!" when not to shout "Heil Hitler!" was penalized by death. He stood in the face of an onrushing storm, which swept others to the guillotine, the chopman's block—standing in the name of Him who said, "I am with you even unto the end . . ."

He saw heads roll from the block as the Hitler-ax came down. He heard the *rat-a-tat-tat* of machine gun fire as row upon row of Jews, lining the walls of Hitler's hate, were murdered. He saw men purged; some beaten insensible; some starved to living corpses; some nailed alive in boxes slowly to die. He heard the groans of those in dungeons, listened to the wail of mothers separated from sons, caught the moans of parents as they saw their fifteen-year-old daughters being sent to Hitler camps where they were to breed Hitler's super-race.

He saw . . . heard . . . listened, knowing well that Hitler who thus could degrade a nation, destroy a people, had the power of life and death over his own body—yet was assured that this Hitler had no power to touch his soul.

This is Martin Niemoeller—tough-fibered like men who walked triumphantly into lions' dens, who sang gloriously as the torch of a Nero was slung at their oil-soaked bodies.

Well did his father Heinrich name him Martin, for this Niemoeller was to become a second Martin Luther, achieving again for his nation what Luther did for sixteenth-century Germany. Like the first Martin who faced the pope and his armies, this second Martin stands against the man who epitomizes all which the pope and his cohorts were.

In the new order Hitler, acting as God's understudy, cries out, "The Church that fights me, I shall annihilate." Against such onslaughts Niemoeller stood in his pulpit and sang, "A mighty fortress is our God," which has long been the battle charge for Christians sired by Luther, who also wrote the song.

As Luther before him, Niemoeller draws his strength from a faith which is founded upon the Bible as the inspired Word of God. "Where would he find his place?" asks Paul Hutchinson in the *Atlantic Monthly*. ". . . a sermon by Martin Niemoeller would be found to rest on the old premise that the Bible is the literally inspired Word of God, to be regarded as fully authoritative in all its parts for all ages."

This second Martin is the son of the first, and he looks upon the doctrinal statements and Christian Confessions, penned in the sixteenth century, as sufficient for this day. For him the creed of Luther needs no alteration in order to make it serve as the congenial doctrinal foundation for the mind of this century.

Nor would he insist that Christianity demonstrate its worth by stepping to the fore in the solution of community problems. Christianity to Niemoeller is a God-given entity, which centers in Jesus Christ, and only the Hitler-inspired German Church, with its so-called "positive Christianity," based upon a rewritten Bible, is thus concerned.

This "Hitlerized Christianity" would remake the world through force, blitzkrieg, panzer divisions, luftwaffes. As Luther before him, Niemoeller would transform the world through the Kingdom of God, as Christ so proclaimed.

And for this faith, as the first Martin, he is ready to die. Let's trace his story, into which the elements of drama and tragedy are brewed. It is all there:

the hero becomes the incarnation of that which Hitler hates and seeks to destroy. For this national hero to have become a national martyr links him more closely with Luther.

"Nature has made it impossible for him to reach his goal by compromise," writes the author of *Martin Niemoeller und sein Bekenntnis,* a book published in Switzerland and banned in Martin's native land. When a U-boat captain in the first World War there was no compromise in his fighting spirit and on stepping into the pulpit, after being spiritually transformed by the Master, he could stand no less firmly for conscience, God and right than he had previously fought for country and hearth.

For Martin Niemoeller, life really began when his childhood dream of entering the German navy, first dawning upon him at the age of five, was realized in his eighteenth year. Personally in all his written works he seldom, if ever, lifts the curtain on his early life. Occasionally in his *From U-Boat to Pulpit* he allows us to glimpse those pre-U-boat days when he was a youngster in his father's parsonage.

Life for Martin was always a battle, fighting either under the navy flag or the Christian banner, and he had little time for frolicsome rambles through memory's long lane that led back to his native Westphalia. When he did thus reminisce it was in the times when U-boat battles had been swallowed up in the German defeat and his soul was wallowing in the sloughs of despondency.

God endowed him with a noble heritage, and from infancy placed him in an atmosphere with a piety which might well have sprung from Martin Luther's own home. His father Heinrich Niemoeller was a Lutheran minister, serving under the State Church, and was noted not so much for intellectual superiority as for his approachable humanness. A genial personage, he was always popular with his parishioners, and even to the end of his long life, which came on March 23, 1941 in his eighty-second year, he was in demand for christenings, weddings and funerals.

In his own right Father Niemoeller was a great and furious preacher. He did not leave all the Hitler-fighting to his famous son Martin. Long since retired when Martin was imprisoned, old Heinrich stepped back into the pulpit and thundered his favorite sermon on "The Bible is not Bound," from one end of Germany to the other. When the Nazis placed their preachers in the established churches Heinrich found himself without a pulpit, and so, with others, he engaged a dance hall of his city and packed it to the doors.

He conducted what many called a one-man preaching mission throughout his nation, after Martin's voice was stilled in the concentration camp. When Ewart Edmund Turner, former minister of the American Church in Berlin, asked him what his favorite text would be, had he but one to offer, he reached for a massive copy of the Luther Bible, saying, "This would be my text." When asked to be more specific, he said, "Jeremiah 29:11-14, especially the eleventh verse."

"For I know the thoughts that I think toward you ... thoughts of peace ... to give you an expected end. (*Das Ich eauch gebe das Ende, dess ihr wartet*)."

He closed the conversation charging Dr. Turner that when he returned to America no one should be allowed to pity the father and mother of Martin Niemoeller but rather to pity the follower of Christ who knows not the joy that is set before those who endure the cross, despising the shame thereof.

He concluded, "It is terrible to have a son in a concentration camp. Paula and I know that. But there would be something more terrible for us: *if God had needed a faithful martyr and our Martin had been unwilling.*"

In his Elberfeld parish, though out of a church in which to proclaim the truth, Father Niemoeller, as he is happily called, found a larger congregation than at any time in his glory-kissed and trouble-marked career. He realized even to his last that with Martin in a concentration camp, he and his other preacher-son, Wilhelm, must defend the Christian truth as they and Martin saw it.

From Paula, Martin inherited much of his facial features, but from Heinrich came the aptness in making the Scriptures become vibrant through an application to life situations, a human-wide capacity for personal intimacy with people, and what the Germans term a Westphalian thick skull . . . German hardheadedness—a complete enwrapment in a task until it is finished, however difficult the path or thorny the crown.

Through the years of Martin's home life the father served two parishes, the first at Lippstadt, in Westphalia, and the second at Elberfeld, where he completed his militant Christian ministry by entering the Church Triumphant on a wind-tossed Sunday of

March, 1941. Martin was born at the first-named place on January 14, 1892. Father Heinrich brought to Martin in those early years a character geniality, while Mother Paula loved and blessed him with a generous affection. Each though stern knew how to be tender, and in the guidance of Martin's young life their steady hands were not far from his growing personality.

Lutheran piety marked the home, while parental sternness bounded it. In his early pulpit days Martin lifts a grateful voice for daily Bible readings in Heinrich's parsonage and tells us that they helped to direct his own devotional life. Father Niemoeller, a strict German Lutheran, was never influenced by the modern criticism of the Bible, a familiar background of current religion in Germany.

His sermons followed the Lutheran order of services, and his credo did not go beyond Luther's doctrinal statements. The beautiful German of Luther's Bible, which gave life, depth and picturesque aliveness to modern German, rang in little Martin's ears daily, and the sermonic food upon which he fed for his first eighteen years was the substantial religious fare of one tutored in Lutheran history and acquainted with confessional literature.

It is natural that when the popular submarine captain became the dynamic Lutheran preacher his sermons also should ride the broad current of Christian certainty and herald salvation by faith, the doctrine upon which Martin Luther founded Protestantism.

The Lippstadt congregation, during Martin's preschool days, made the Niemoeller parsonage church headquarters, and a constant stream of the people of this influential congregation flowed through its portals. Martin thus became so accustomed to a home flooded with youth and vibrant with parish problems that in his Munster theolog days he laments the fact he had been able to gather no youth about him, a defect which in his Dahlem pastorate in Berlin was to be amply rectified.

All of Martin's school days were spent at Elberfeld, an industrial section, where the congregation was made up of workmen in factories and shops. It was here at five that the great dream of his life possessed his childhood soul. He aspired to a navy career, and naught was able to hold him from this goal.

Later in speaking of the gentle yet firm influences of Heinrich and Paula upon his life, he refers to the fact that they did not restrain this ambition to captain a navy vessel. Even though, he tells us, it was their natural desire that he should follow in his father's footsteps and enter the ministry, they did not try to alter the set of his own mental sail that steered him in the end to a U-boat command.

Tugging at his youthful consciousness was a pulpit career. It hovered over him in an undefinable manner, breaking into mental spotlight time and again. Here is an example which springs from the fluctuating fates of his submarine operations. He had been busily engaged in destroying commerce, and wirelessed his Flotilla, "UC67 has completed minelaying operations; three steamers totaling seventeen thousand tons sunk."

Victory had marked his work. He was again playing hide-and-seek with American and British de-

stroyers, outwitting Italian battleships. In the midst
of such activities, he was on the bridge standing
watch with a fellow-officer named Topp. Conversation rambled on through the quirks of fate, not
knowing at what moment they should be required to
make a crash dive, or command No. 1 tube to fire.
Suddenly talking winds shifted to the thought of
having to change their vocations, for already it was
September of that fateful 1918, and each was certain
Germany could not win.

"We were both engaged to be married," he says in
rethinking the incident in 1934 from the heights of
his famous Dahlem-Berlin pastorate. "I hardly know
how we get onto the idea of having to change our
vocation; neither do I know how it comes about that
I suddenly decide, 'Then I will be a parson!' Since
the age of five I had never thought of any profession
but the sea, to which I was passionately attached."

Yet that aurora of being a parson swung like a
tapestry from the walls of his mind, where it had
been hung by the faithful life of his parson-father
Heinrich.

When confirmation age arrived, the event was
more than a passing religious ceremony to the youthful Martin who stood poised on the grandest hills of
life that overlook adolescence. He had been carefully
tutored by Heinrich, father-vicar. The rite made
such a lasting imprint on his life that during his submarine days he tells us that it threw about him a
constraining influence which caused him to remain
true to the vows taken at the time.

The act, charged with the Divine, was to him a
soul-redeeming experience from which he could not
escape. Confirmation became transformation.

Finishing the Elberfeld schools at the age of eighteen, Heinrich and Paula decided to assist him in attaining the goal of his ambition, and accordingly arranged for him to enter the Naval Academy at Kiel, which automatically brought him into the navy.

He became a cadet on the old cruiser "Hertha," and in 1910, among other trips, visited the Mediterranean, only to recall when his first submarine, the "U73," entered the same sea during the war in 1916 that many of his "Hertha" shipmates had already found watery graves. During the same year he shipped to Pola, in the Adriatic, and for the first time visited a British warship, many of which he was to encounter a few years later when the war broke out.

The following year he was a junior midshipman, and during a leave of absence spent several weeks with his grandparents in Westerkappeln. "And when the time came for me to depart," he tells us, "I felt quite tearful." It was a parting which to him somewhat partook of the character of an expulsion from the Garden of Eden.

Even during his later ministerial student days, leave-taking from Westerkappeln was a heart rending experience. There he found quiet grandparents, friendly neighbors and rural calm a delightful contrast to cadeting on a cruiser or studying naval strategy at Kiel.

But he was on his way and happily satisfied. When the World War broke there was action with all the fury of blasting guns, belching cannon, sinking ships. Now it was Lieutenant Niemoeller who on the "Thuringen" took part in raids on the British coast. He was with the German fleet in battle exercises in

Heligoland Bight, and engaged in an attack in the Gulf of Riga.

During the second year of the war the High Seas Fleet lost the battle initiative, and Lieutenant Martin, with other young officers, believed it would see no further action. The Imperial was a grand fleet, he thought, but one doomed to defeat. His ship, the "Thuringen," a twenty-three-thousand-ton vessel, was moored, and impatiently he felt he was wasting his time on the quarter-deck as a watch-keeper when by the thousands his comrades-in-arms were dying on the battlefields or losing their lives in destroyed U-boats.

He craved action . . . wanted to be in battle . . . dreamed of submarine warfare, only to be denied these privileges. Then came career-altering October, 1915, when the captain sent for him. Walking with high spirit he went before his commander to be told that he had been appointed for submarine duty the first of December.

At last his opportunity had come, though he affirms that when his old ship was coaling in Wilhelms- haven, and he took leave the last of November, it was with a pang. "I now left behind me the happiest days of my youth," he says writing in his native tongue. ". . . the grim realities of war were to begin for me."

He was to record submarine history to his credit— tragic for British and American shipping, but glori- ous for his nation. He made such history that when German defeat came, he was one of the nation's popular heroes—a position, a fame which, when his pulpit days were to begin, gave him a grip upon the hearts of his countrymen. God began thus to weave

the fabric of his personality into the warp and woof
of the Fatherland so that on the striking of the Divine
hour Niemoeller's Hitler-defiance pumped courage
into the sagging hearts of fellow-Christians to such
an alluring extent that one-eighth of the German
pastors and their congregations followed him into
battle for conscience and right.

CHAPTER II

PLAYING HIDE-AND-SEEK WITH BATTLESHIPS

HE had sought action and now was soon to be hurled into submarine warfare. First came two months of training at the Eckernfoerde submarine school, where he was instructed in such intricacies of submarines as automatic vents, crash dives, blowers and trimming pumps, diving tanks, periscopes, torpedo firing and minelaying. When he was turned out a full-fledged submarine officer, he was assigned to the "U73", an old and recently commissioned submarine minelayer, which had far more liabilities than assets.

She was popularly known as the "floating coffin." Her speed was a tragically slow 9.5 knots on the surface which was cut to four when submerged. When everything worked, Lieutenant Martin informs us, they could dive in two minutes; "but all too often everything did not work." Her 3.5 inch gun, mounted on the conning tower, necessitated a stern-on turn to shell an enemy vessel. With both torpedo tubes fitted outboard, even a slightly rolling sea made it impossible to service the death-dealing, ship-destroying torpedoes. In this minelayer, aspiring Martin went forth to battle.

When April of 1916 broke, the "U73" with its crew sailed for the Mediterranean with the command to lay mines off hostile ports and in the narrow fairways where enemy shipping was carried on. Tricky North Sea weather revealed many unpredictable characteristics of the submarine. The gyro compass could not take the pitching and rolling of the ship, which forced the officers, like it or no, to sail by the drift of the currents and the rule of thumb.

Added to this defect was a constantly growing list of sick crewmen, until the well half of the crew were forced to care for the sick half. In the midst of rolling sea, bad weather, sick crew, when the periscope was up or the submarine surfaced, steamers could be seen coming and going; but the weather made it impossible for them to submerge and fire torpedoes.

On April 12, however, luck favored them and the "Inverlyon", a large vessel, was sighted. The sub surfaced, and firing a warning shot, the ship hove to. The crew, sensing death, took to lifeboats while the "U73" tried to sink her by gunfire. The heavy sea made this difficult, but a dozen shots finally sent the ship to the bottom.

On through to the Mediterranean the U-boat went, battling its way through difficulties. It was on this trip that Boatswain's Mate Hennig called out, "Man overboard!" When the submarine slowed, Niemoeller was able to see a swimmer's head bobbing in the waves. Circling to come nearer the drowning shipmate, a man leaped into the water with a line in his hand and swam toward the now unconscious seaman.

"The seconds seem like eternity . . . both are hauled aboard by strong arms . . . stiff and lifeless," relates the lieutenant, adding, "the second within five days." After trying artificial respiration on the drowned person, the captain gave up hope. But the boatswain's mate kept pumping and pumping for forty, fifty minutes, and "actually the drowned man breathes," and is alive, though weak and corpselike.

Bringing this man back from the brink of death made a lasting impression upon Niemoeller, and on looking at him he tingled with a strange sensation and thought: the man brought back from the dead.

Around Lisbon the "U73" laid mines and steamed through the Straits of Gibraltar, hiding now beneath the waves, surfacing and crash diving to avoid the lurking battleships of the enemy. Once in the distance a steamer took shape and laid its course parallel to that of the sub, and when engine trouble caused Niemoeller's ship to stop because of a faulty suction inlet in the pumps, the other ship followed suit.

The steamer kept calling by wireless but the sub was not able to decode the message. Only through the subterfuge of hoisting the British white ensign were they able to shake the unwelcomed enemy ship from their course. The officers stood by to crash dive at any moment. Toward evening another large steamer was met, and their courses were laid in such a manner that they would cross within a few hundred feet of each other. Things looked awkward and became serious when the ship turned broadside and the submarine officers recognized it as a British battleship with heavy guns.

"Diving stations!" came the command, and shortly the "U73" went down to sixty feet, circled to the north and outwitted the navy vessel.

A few days later the submarine surfaced early in the morning, and Martin was awakened with the cry, "We are being fired upon!" They had come upon a small vessel which with the ping of death had opened fire. Throughout the day they "dived and dodged a number of pursuers round Cape Bon," which was one of the hottest spots in the entire Mediterranean, and hove on to safety amid stormy waters.

Minelaying was interspered with outwitting destroyers until they came to Valetta Harbor, the enemy stronghold, where mine after mine was dropped in front of this most important British Mediterranean naval base. Throughout the day a careful watch was kept on the bridge while the ship's company stood by at diving stations.

Came the cry that night, "Destroyer to port!" A half mile on the beam Niemoeller saw a destroyer come creeping out of the night, which flashed signals at the sub. The alarm bell sounded, "Action stations!" and the command was given, "Open vents." Slowly the water gurgled into the diving tanks, the conning-tower hatch was closed, and the depth gauge pointer set at a hundred feet. Breathlessly the crew awaited the thunder of guns and the dread explosion of depth bombs, but nothing happened. By one o'clock that day the twenty-second mine was laid and the "U73" had finished her orders.

On the return journey to Kiel, minelaying done, they sighted a British warship which steered a zigzag course to evade lurking submarines. The old and asthmatic "U73" being too slow to intercept her, they satisfied themselves by cutting a trough through the waves for the home port. The sub's radio picked up a wireless, "Battleship 'Russel' . . . struck a mine in the Mediterranean; 124 men missing; 676 saved."

This was the first direct news they had received of the effectiveness of their mines—many others, however, to follow.

After a respite at Kiel, where the submarine was refitted and made shipshape, the second time it nosed its way toward the Mediterranean, with the parting shout from the docks, "Good luck and good hunting!" The objective was to render the Gulf of Salonica and the Ægean in general unsafe for enemy shipping through a bristle-thick distribution of mines.

On July 31, 1916, they slipped into the Gulf of Salonica, and in the late afternoon they surfaced to ventilate the ship. Due to the great visibility and the nearness of land, they always kept submerged by daylight, doing their work under cover of darkness.

During the night two steamers were sighted, but due to the fact that the sub's exhaust was throwing out showers of sparks in its smoke, the commander dared not attack the vessels. At midnight they were forced to crash dive to avoid being sniped at by a destroyer. A before-dawn surfacing assisted the captain in plotting his course, and at five in the morning they quietly sailed underseas toward the port. At eight-thirty the first mine was laid, and by ten, eighteen were dropped without arousing suspicion on the part of the patrolling destroyer.

All day the "U73" remained submerged. The sub's atmosphere became dense and foul, with the temperature dipping beyond the hundred mark's horizon. The numerous small craft and lazing patrol boats made it impossible for them to surface during daylight, which required a constant flow of oxygen to be released in the submarine. After fifteen hours thus underseas, on opening the conning-tower hatch, the first breath of fresh air was as welcome to the sailors as a sight of their sweetest home-port girls.

"The first breath of air . . . after fifteen hours on the bottom," exults Martin, "is an experience never to be forgotten." By now the submarine had the sea to itself, and so they all swelled their lungs with midnight-freshness brewed in the balmy Mediterranean, much to the joyous elation of the day-stifled crew.

Daylight revealed enemy ships near by, and a noisy cruiser within torpedo range. So close they were that Niemoeller's sub could expose its periscope for only a few seconds at a time. No. 1 torpedo tube was prepared to fire as they approached the cruiser. Orders barked out with machine gun rapidity:

"No. 1 tube, stand by!—Up periscope!—No. 1 tube, *fire!—Down periscope!* . . ."

They crash dived and Martin counted the seconds . . . thirty . . . thirty-one . . . thirty-two . . . and with a thunderous belch the explosion rent the bay. A hit, and up shot the periscope. There listing to starboard was the cruiser in a cloud of white steam. Nor were the other vessels inactive. Shells began to explode around the "U73," and she went down to eighty feet in a crash dive. Overhead Niemoeller could hear the whirr of pursuing vessels, among which utmost confusion existed.

The captain ordered, "Stand by to lay mines!" While steaming out of the bay they dropped a batch of six mines across their path. Astern they heard a loud explosion, and Martin relates that as the submarine went down to a hundred and thirty feet the crew felt a little easier, only to encounter bad luck in the form of a No. 2 leaky tank.

Until four that afternoon the "U73" sailed submerged, and when they shot the periscope up for a brief look-around, the officer saw a destroyer shortly astern. This, however, they were able to shake from their wet tail, so that during the night two more mine barrages were dumped in the Mudros Bay, and "having got rid of all mines, we make for home."

This return trip proved to be an obstacle race, for shortly in the South Ægean the port propeller shaft was cracked, and the next day the starboard engine gave way altogether. The weather was so heavy that it was virtually impossible for the seamen to keep their feet, from being sea-tossed like bowling pins; and Martin remarks, "We were all fed up with the long underwater trip . . . " Added to this was the luckless thought that they had to get through the serious Otranto Straits with a partially disabled ship.

The lieutenant tells us that they were fortunate in getting there at all, for at daybreak on August 9, a destroyer appeared on their starboard quarter and made for them at wave-crashing speed. Due to the sub's smoky exhaust, which at night trailed behind a shower of sparks, they had been unable to spot the destroyer until she was less than a half-mile away.

When the order, "Action stations!" belled out, they got down to sixty feet only by the damp skin of their conning tower. They heard the destroyer's propellers whirring above them, and this was so loud that they could catch the sound "even without putting our ears to the boat's side." Death rode those waves, but underneath the sea was Martin with a destiny-controlled charm.

As those shrill bells blared out, "Action stations!" for Martin it came to have a foreboding meaning. Each one seemed to sound the death knell of his last hour, and when they bellowed in the sub's internals, his soul revolted with each jangle that cut with an icy knife down through his spine.

Sweet revenge soon peeped over the U-boat's snout, for the next evening they torpedoed an Italian schooner, which proved to be even "groggier" than the submarine.

Back to Pola's dockyards they sped, for the rheumatic "U73" direly called for doctoring. Here Martin welcomed heartening news in the form of British steamers, troop ships and a cruiser falling prey to one of the submarine's mines.

The shipshape "U73" was ready for action by the end of October, and they headed for the Straits of Otranto, on which trip she was more than busy dodging five lines of patrols. They also encountered pairs of drifters, which towed explosive sweeps with a vain hope of snaring a sub. Martin looked upon the devices more as a tiresome interruption than as a menace. He did, however, learn to respect the high-speed British destroyers, each of which might have meant death to him and his shipmates.

November and December were spent in petulant minelaying operations, unsuccessful attempts to torpedo ships, with little knowledge of their victories until they learned that the fifty-thousand-ton "Britannic," pride of the British mercantile marine, had fallen prey to a mine barrage which their "floating coffin" had laid. Similarly the "Burdigala," a French cruiser, had gone to the bottom.

A few days later Martin heard of serious Allied shipping losses in the Ægean, "altogether about ninety thousand tons." He notes, "The floating coffin is paying her way."

After a Pola dockyard refit, Martin's ship was once more detailed for action in the western Mediterranean, and during the 1916 Christmas season the submarine was busy laying mines off Port Said and Alexandria, and, when occasion came, destroying commerce in the same sectors.

When December 21 arrived, all hope of spending Christmas at the base was given up. This brought a tinge of regret to Niemoeller, who remarked, " 'Peace on earth' may yet be managed if the war goes on long enough," suggesting that there was once a Thirty Years' War, and perhaps this one might last that long.

On the 22nd, at eleven-thirty, Martin sighted a tanker with its escorts. Orders were given to fire No. 1 tube, and back came the report, "Hit amidships! —Down periscope." And in the fore compartment the phonograph played *Deutschland, Deutschland uber alles!* which in his war journal he henceforth notes marks all direct hits. But the battle was not over, for five minutes later when the periscope lifted, one of the trawlers tried hard to ram the "U73," which crash dived to a hundred and thirty feet.

Niemoeller and his shipmates welcomed midnight with eight depth charges which a racing battleship from Alexandria dropped on them. Again Providence was with the submarine and its human cargo, and with little more than a severe shaking the explosives let them off.

By Christmas they were near Crete, where they accosted a Greek ship, but due to a cracked propeller on the port side, and a dead engine on the other, they had to give up the hunt, with only the starboard electric motor used to keep the "U73" pointed on her course.

That was a dreary Christmas, though Mate Hennig climbed through the bulkhead door and shouted, "It's Christmas, sir!" and immediately put up an eight-inch Christmas tree, made of matchwood, green dyed straw and red-headed pins. Notwithstanding wars, tumult, pain and bloodshed, the Christmas spirit still lived!

In the depth of the Mediterranean, on his bunk in that creaky old U-boat, Niemoeller got out his Confirmation Bible and read the Gospels for the occasion, a sense of gratitude flooding his spirit as he relived in imagination those stirring events when long ago the angels had sung, "Good will toward men," though at the time, good will seemed a chimerical wisp of fate.

The "U73" showed her disrespect for the Yuletide spirit by developing a serious case of lubricating troubles, consuming on that day two hundred and seventy gallons of their dwindling oil supplies. To top the occasion, six of the crew were bunked by high fevers.

The following day Martin remarks that with the dregs of his morning tea (so scarce was their water) he managed to lather his face for his first shave in three weeks.

The "U73," an utter wreck, promptly limped back to Pola and tied up alongside the mother ship, "Gaea," which was steamheated, and "all made a rush for the bathrooms." This was to be Niemoeller's last voyage with the submarine which had shown him his first year's war activity in a submersible.

Her history had already largely been written, for it took almost a year for the dockyard hands to put her in sailing order again. In early 1918 he saw action on the Palestine front, and without a pang in his heart Martin affirms that "we sank her at the end of October, 1918, by means of explosive charges a couple of miles from Pola," that she might not fall into Italian hands.

Dawning 1917 saw the Emperor's peace proposals refused by the Allies—and created a problem for Niemoeller. As the New Year came in, Martin racked his brain "how to get another appointment . . . Nothing to do but carry on. I was too junior to get a command of my own." He tells us that he lacked just six months more submarine service as a watchkeeper to get his own command. The immediate aim on his agenda was to get this experience.

The opportunity greeted him sooner than he expected when the captain of the "U39" came into the room where Martin was and lamented the fact that his navigating officer had broken his arm in a fall. "My boat is under orders to sail early in January," he said, "and there is only one navigating officer per boat and the captains are unwilling to part with theirs." At once Martin broke in, pleading for a chance at the position, "How about signing me on?" The captain was reluctant in that the lieutenant lacked much of the qualifying training and experience. But in the end the Lieutenant Commander in charge gave his permission. "I looked upon these accidents as the hand of fate," says Niemoeller, in checking back through his career as God led him, during those U-boat days, to the pulpit.

With a few days to rub up on his rusty navigation and to renew acquaintance with the *Nautical Almanac,* he set about preparing himself for this position. He also made a study of the "U39's" two chronometers, for the new boat was vastly superior to his old ship, and her devilish mechanisms were more alluringly intricate.

Action began on January 9 when their first torpedo was fired at a steamer with a direct hit. Martin soon discovered that the British had learned a new trick or two since the previous summer. They were hunting subs with hydrophones, to pick up the engine rumble, "and when they think themselves close enough their depth charges are to be taken more seriously than the 'poppers' of the last summer."

His daily schedule ran something like this: At dawn he worked out their position from the stars. In the forenoon he shot the sun, at noon to take their sight; and again in the afternoon he shot the sun. In the evening he took their position from the stars, provided, of course, they were visible. Between times he logged out course and position and alterations of speed. "Neither must I forget to wind the chronometers."

He thought all this instructive and interesting, with a chuckle that the Imperial German Navy was not sent out on a month's cruise in the Mediterranean during the World War just for the fun of teaching a junior lieutenant navigation.

At the time he was twenty-five, with the sap of life running full course, and there were few tricks of the U-boat trade which escaped his notice. For when those six months of navigation were up with the "U39," he dreamed of his own command, and as the hour arrived he wanted to be fully prepared.

On January 25 two ships were sighted with a convoy of three French destroyers, marking thus the high value of their cargo. Forstmann, their commander, stood by the conning tower, with Niemoeller cramped beside him, noting every word and movement, and the officer, already wearing the *Pour le merite,* prepared to carry out the attack in copybook style. "Everything goes off as by the drill book, but in deadly earnestness and seriousness," Martin says. Course and speed were altered to suit the shifting pace of the convoy.

There, not sixty yards on the flank, passed a French destroyer. Forstmann commanded: "Slow ahead both!" then took a quick look at the torpedo sight on the periscope, whispering to Martin, " A troop ship . . . Up periscope!—No. 1 tube, ready." Pushing his cap on the back of his head, the commanding officer took a quick periscope peep and said, "Fire! Down to a hundred."

A twenty-seconds' pause was followed by the rumble of an explosion. A direct hit. Ten minutes later they upped the periscope and saw the ship rapidly sinking, with a destroyer standing by to salvage the survivors.

That sinking troop ship planted a foot of tragical imprint upon the mental neck of the lieutenant's

mind, for as the destroyer was picking up the sur-
viving soldiers, the periscope rammed its snout
through the waters, which attracted the destroyer's
fire. But, as Martin notes, a periscope is a tiny thing,
and the fire was ineffectual. So in order to hamper
the rescue as much as possible, the submarine darted
about sticking up here and yon its gleaming snout,
though unable to fire another hell-bent torpedo.

"When the troop ship had sunk," he says with a
somewhat dejected note breaking through his German
record of the event, "we make for home, as we
originally intended."

But in the ward room pros and cons flew about
among the crew and officers on the debatable subject:
*Were we justified in stopping the Frenchman from
carrying out his task of rescue?* There were good
arguments for and against, but let them shuttle back
and forth as they might, Niemoeller appends to his
original record these words, "We cannot feel com-
fortable about it . . ."

This threw on the screen of their minds the com-
plex idea and problem of modern warfare, inspired
by a single experience such as Martin had just blazed
through. He recalled the then-current talk in theological circles of a "moratorium on Christianity."
As junior officers they knew nothing and cared less
about such talk of dogmatic topics. But he could not
escape the thought of spiritual bankruptcy resulting
from such actions, when officers and men were forced
to destroy life wherein it was utterly "impossible to
maintain a clear conscience."

That January 25 became a turning point in his
career, for he realized the inexorable impossibility and

time-wide improbability of building a moral universe. He decided that all the talk on a moratorium on Christianity merely presaged a moral collapse through which civilization was then tramping its blood-stained way.

Two days later on rejoining his old "U73" at Pola he wore his Iron Cross I with a feeling of having earned it by engaging in a prescribed number of successful operations, though his soul was seared by the events. As the submarine was declared unseaworthy, he was ordered to Tondern for a special course in code deciphering. Though the work, consisting mainly of instruction by deep-brained mathematicians, was interesting, it held no positive elation. For he detested "pen pushing," as he designated his new task.

Later he was assigned to replace a junior civil officer of the Mediterranean admiralty division. Though his assignments were valuable and instructive and not at all boring, he could not rid himself of the feeling that he was merely getting out orders, "young squirt that I was," for the senior commanding officers, upon whom he looked with admiration.

This "pen pushing" in the end took him to Berlin, where his staff daily received admiralty reports from army headquarters through General Ludendorff, and gave him an inside track on the military and naval secrets of the war.

Later in appraising those two months in the Kaiserin Augusta Strasse, he sensed that they had been of utmost importance in the shaping of his future life. He learned how to appraise isolated incidents as re-

lated to wider issues, and "to think strategically in
the place of tactically."

When the Hitler days came up and he stood forth
as commander-in-chief of a new Christian battalion,
which faced the Hitlerized Germanic religion, "this
experience stood me in good stead regarding my own
destiny," and that of the Confessional Church to
which his boldness and faith gave birth.

The Berlin job implanted a time-altering footprint
on his life in another sphere as well. The oldest sister
of his former classmate Hermann Bremer was studying in Berlin at the time, and it came about quite
naturally that they renewed a childhood friendship by
spending their free Sunday afternoons sailing on the
Wannsee or Havel. This brought about an exchange
of letters and a year later ended in their engagement.

No greater blessing has come to Martin through the
years than the young lady Else Bremer he thus met in
Berlin, for as his wife she skylighted his purposes
when he was a theolog in Munster, stood by him
through the bombings of their home in Dahlem,
strengthened his faith during his arrest and trial, and
now, while incarcerated in a concentration camp, her
bi-monthly letters and regular, though infrequent,
visits are the bright and sustaining dynamics of his life.

In the building of this Martin Niemoeller, to become
the second Luther for the religious leadership of Hitlerized Germany, there must be those long and tedious
climbs toward submarine command that he in the
end might be prepared to lead, marshall the hosts of
the Confessional Church to which he was to give birth.

It was spring, warm and sunny, in Berlin, when he
received orders from Commander Kophamel to pack

his traps, "for in the morning we are off to Kiel." Not certain what was in the bag for him, he hoped it would be his own command, only to learn that he was to be first lieutenant on the "U151," sister ship to the well-known "Deutschland."

This wrought consternation in his mental luggage, for already by then his 1910 cadet classmates held commands in small submarines or many of them had already gone to the bottom in their own ships, while he, as he terms it, was playing "second dickey."

A promise, however, brightened his mental horizon: after one cruise in the Mediterranean his own U-boat awaited him. And with a light heart he set out for his first lieutenancy, which position he found to be only that of a glorified "maid of all work, with lots to be done."

CHAPTER III

UP PERISCOPE!

THROUGHOUT the rest of Niemoeller's submarine career, during which he not only served as first lieutenant on another's ship but captained his own as well, he engaged in hair-raising and devil-may-care episodes. He matched wits with quick-brained destroyer-commanders and hair-trigger-fingered gun crews, and often as not outmaneuvered them. There were, however, many occasions on which he escaped death only through a kind providence which saved his life for a fate nobler than filling a watery grave in the sea's belly.

His first engagement on the "U151" was a near-miss by a destroyer which bordered on fatality, and had the new ship been as aged in her joints and as phlegmatic in her engines as the old one, they would never have escaped. The new sub was the latest word in fighting under-water equipment, over which a number one crew kept vigil.

They had barely set out in early August, when the captain was presiding at lunch in the ward room, which left Niemoeller in charge. Not suspecting lurking danger, Martin unzealously guarded the conning tower. Giving the command to "Up periscope!" he took a quick look around, when looming large on the horizon was a new destroyer on steam trial heading arrow-straight for them. She was clipping the knots off at a gallant speed. There was no time to maneuver out of her way, nor had she noticed the periscope. Martin shouted, "Flood all tanks, lie on the bottom!"

The flood valves reluctantly opened and the water gurgled into the regulating tank. Commanded the officer of the day, "Stop both! Down periscope!" and with a thud at sixty-five feet the submarine crouched on the sandy bottom, while overhead the whirr of the passing destroyer's propellers churned the seas.

Had Martin been a moment slower in sighting the steam-snorting destroyer, the submarine would have been rammed amidship. But that lightning-quick decision saved the ship and all lives aboard as well. He learned that often his life depended upon quick decisions that cut through his volition with the keenness of a scimitar.

Near-death stalked the "U151," for on her next engagement with an enemy ship she escaped destruction only through a miracle. Early in the 1917 September when the U-boat menace was at its height, Niemoeller's sub was off the Shetlands. They were lunching on macaroni and bacon at the time in the ward room, when the report came from the bridge, "Smoke on the port beam!" The captain wiped his mouth and left while the others finished their meal.

Surfacing, the submarine recognized the ship as a small steamer, and approached within eight thousand yards and opened fire. The steamer turned south when suddenly an answering gun flash was seen. They engaged in a running gunfight, though the smaller calibered shells of the steamer's guns dropped short of the U-boat. After a half-hour or so the sub managed a direct hit in the enemy's boiler rooms. Clouds of white smoke filled the air and

Niemoeller saw lifeboats being lowered. The captain ordered the submarine to proceed carefully to within a mile of the ship.

Suddenly three salvos flashed from the enemy's guns, the final shot hitting its target. Already the order to crash dive had been given and Martin was in the act of closing the hatch cover when the shot landed on the sub's tough hide. He was knocked down into the conning tower, but managed to close the armored deadlights over the scuttles.

A large chunk of steel hit the hatch cover and jammed it open, while Martin noticed flying fragments around the forward gun. "Then the water closed over us as the boat shivers under the impact of the fourth salvo," he relates. They go down at a violent rate of speed, with water pouring into the U-boat through the jammed conning-tower hatch . . . a hundred feet . . . a hundred and thirty . . . a hundred and sixty.

Commanded the captain, "Stand by to blow!—Blow all tanks!" Martin watched the depth needle stop and then begin to rise, when orders stopped the blowers; for the submarine dared not surface. The crew raced forward and then aft to trim the boat and maintain it at a constant depth. "A veritable devil's dance," Martin characterized the acts.

Later when the periscope was raised, the sea was seen to be clear, and on surveying the damage, it was unbelievable that a U-boat could have suffered so severely and not have been destroyed. The conning-tower hatch was damaged; where the bridge was on the tower, all had been wrecked; one of the "Winona's" shells had gone completely through both sides of the armored ammunition trunk, finally to

burst under the bridge; another shell had destroyed
the left-hand gunsight and bracket of the forward
six-inch gun; a third had penetrated the upper deck
superstructure.

More serious than all were the tell-tale yellow
stains from the poisonous fumes of ammunition,
stowed below the upper deck, which the British had
hit. The shells were shattered and picric acid
smeared the deck.

Checking through this amazing amount of damage,
Martin exclaimed, ". . . a marvel the shells had not
detonated. A near thing." And back of that marvel
was the guiding hand of God, which safely bore
Niemoeller through every danger that he might stand
as a mighty witness to the unchangeableness of the
Christian message.

Shortly, however, a joyous note rode the wireless
reports—that the "Winona," the damage-dealing
ship, had finally been bagged by a German submarine.

Off Madeira on the last day of September the
"U151" approached within a few miles of a ship and
opened fire. With the first burst of shells, the radio
operator shouted, "German submarine. Hullo! Being shelled. Help for God's sake. Hullo! Hullo!" But
through all the calls for help Martin noticed that the
operator failed to give their position. This he
reckoned as a blessing, for that night a darkened,
and hence enemy, ship hove in sight and was hit
with a torpedo under the bright moonlight.

Just before the ship went down, Martin saw four
lifeboats lowered and sail away. Later the crew
seemed to be returning, so the sub fired a 3.5-
inch shell over them as a warning. Humaneness

caused the captain to permit the sailors return to the vessel, which was kept afloat by her empty holds, and collect their gear before they set off for Portugal.

The submarine's diet had grown monotonous, especially since their potatoes and bread had run out. So with the damaged ship still afloat, the captain and crew boarded it and looked for lubricating oil and fresh fish. The ship's galley was well supplied and the lucky sub-sailors helped themselves to hoards of such fine food as meat, fish, potatoes, vegetables, bread, two barrels of preserved eggs, as well as two cases of export beer.

After collecting food, they sought for linen, part of which was for the ward room and part for cleaning the guns. "Nor did we forget the flags, chronometers and her twelve-pounder gun." The ship's lifesaving raft was ferried from ship to sub all afternoon, filling the U-boat to near-capacity with things which they had been denied.

Martin tells us how on October 12 the bathing problem was solved. Late that evening the captain went to the conning tower while Niemoeller turned in for a night's rest. He was awakened as by a tremendous hand being laid upon the sub's vitals and shaking it with the fury of a raging tempest. Rushing to the captain's assistance, he saw the periscope coming down. Said the other, "He rammed us . . ." —followed by a loud explosion which doused the lights. Everybody crouched in the darkness awaiting the next depth charge, as they supposed. But none came.

Slowly, with several leaks noted, they came up to forty feet when the order was given, "Up periscope."

The captain shook his head . . . Martin seconded him as he looked through the scope. There was nothing in sight! And when they surfaced, not a floating item of the other ship could be found.

When the upper deck cleared, a thirteen-foot hole showed across the sub's stern, and a liberal sprinkling of propeller blades cluttered the hole. Said the captain, "As she rammed us, the destroyer's bottom must have been torn off, and when she sank, her boilers exploded, so that no sign of her remains visible."

And now for the bath. Martin appends, "By keeping the inlet shutter of No. 1 tank open while under weigh, we found the hole made a fine bath with room for at least ten men at a time."—a dangerous expedient which he did not recommend to fellow-sub-officers for procuring a "wash-off" when bathing water ran short.

A couple of days later an intercepted press message reported a United States destroyer missing, and Niemoeller remarked, "We knew where she was."

A few days later the sub again barely escaped destruction. They had torpedoed a ship but failed to register a hit; as the ship gradually pulled out of range a crewman asked permission to fire one of the guns at her. The hit was direct. The ship stopped and the crew hastened to the lifeboats. Martin was unable to decipher the reason, for one hit was not enough to damage the vessel seriously. On drawing nearer he recognized blazes as coming from the vessel, and soon on every side shells were bursting in a veritable shower of explosions.

The lifeboats sailed off, and then every man of the submarine was allowed one shot at the exploding ship. A shot caused red tongues to burst from every hole in the steamer and the deck suddenly broke out in leaping flames. With a terrific detonation and a blast of hot air the ship blew up. Niemoeller leaped off the port side of the conning tower and threw himself face downward on deck.

Showers of shell fragments poured upon the U-boat and its unprotected crew, soon to be engulfed by quietness. On contacting the lifeboats the reason for the explosion was discovered: the cargo consisted of six hundred tons of explosives and three hundred tons of nitroglycerine—almost enough to empty the Atlantic!

Wireless stations on the coast of Morocco had been warned, and submarine chasers came swarming from every nook between Gibraltar and Mogador.

Shortly afterwards while scouring around the Cape Verde Islands and finding pickings slim, the "U151" entered the Porto Grande harbor. On upping the periscope the entire harbor was seen to be filled with ships, two of which furnished torpedo fodder within a few minutes of each other. Then began a chase for the submarine's life, for just behind the sinking steamer a torpedo boat shot forward, and the U-boat had less than sixteen feet of water under its keel. In trying to escape they nearly fouled a Dutch steamer, going down deeper as the harbor permitted. Fortunately the torpedo boat had no depth charges. Expecting the harbor entrance to have been mined, Niemoeller lived in constant fear of an explosion until they were safely out to sea.

On the night of November 21 a steamer came trundling along. On investigation it proved to be a Norwegian ship, the "Johan Mjelde," and was loaded to the gunwales with copper and an assortment of other valuable items. The "U151's" captain decided that the cargo was contraband, and forced the seamen of the captured vessel to assist in loading the submarine with some twenty tons of copper as well as an assortment of such items as cases of cotton underwear, ladies' silk stockings, typewriters, canned salmon and coffee.

Before the loading was completed, three other vessels tipped the horizon with their sails, and their crewmen were also forced to do stevedore work for the "U151." When they could not stow any more on the sub, the job was given up, the hundred seamen placed in their lifeboats and started for land and a torpedo fired at the ship. The shot was a miss, the various lifeboats were rounded up, fire was started in the "Johan Mjelde's" boilers, and she was forced to tow the submarine to the Azores where all the prisoners were landed. Once this operation was completed, the boat was sent to Davy Jones's locker by opening her seacocks.

On the homeward journey early in December the British patrols off the Shetlands caused the U-boat to crash dive down to two hundred and forty feet, where the depth charges, they released, did little more than give the boat a severe knocking about. The event incited no more interest on Niemoeller's part than a short entry in his records, "We pump out the water and gradually peace is restored."

Christmas day, 1917, found the "U151" nearing Kiel, returning from the longest cruise a German submarine ever made: 114 days at sea, 11,400 miles covered and about 50,000 tons of shipping demolished, which included nine steamers, five sailing vessels and one destroyer with seventeen guns.

Early in January of the war's closing year Niemoeller was granted a leave of absence which he spent with his people, "resting and trying to get warm again." This was climaxed by an invitation from the Kaiser for the entire "U151's" crew to spend a month's vacation in Partenkirchen, a resort in the Bavarian mountains. Here Martin found a far different world from the one he had subsisted in for the almost four months' cruise in the sub. There were long and grandly bedecked rambles, winter sports to satiate any young man, "and to top it all excellent fare."

It was more than Martin's soul could stand for so long a time, and he hastened to Elberfeld to enjoy the simplicity of Father Heinrich's parsonage and to catch up on being loved and blessed by Mother Paula. After a short visit to the Berlin admiralty he found himself back in the harness.

And at last, a long last of twenty-one years, his childhood dream came true. In May, 1918, he was given command along with several other junior officers of a new type submarine, the "UC67." He was then twenty-six—having spent eight years in the navy, having been seasoned by various submarine duties and not in the least a stranger to action at sea. He had mastered by experience the tricks in the U-boat's bag and was now ready to sail forth against enemy cargo ships and to challenge the right of hostile battleships to the sea lanes.

The "UC67" was a classy ship, with Diesel engines which gave her a speed of twelve and a half knots. Martin could think of only one thing by which her diving could be described; and he boasted, "She dived like a duck, and was a splendid seaboat."

Action started seriously for the new commander the first of July, and as soon as he found himself off the coast of Italy, at 2:30 A. M. one morning a destroyer was sighted, headed directly toward them. Martin commanded, "Crash dive!"

The duck-diving speed of the "UC67" had an opportunity to show its ability, for barely did she escape the destroyer's keel as it went over the submarine. Plainly the propellers could be heard. The sub's boasted speed had this time been a life-saver, and Martin had occasion to be grateful to a kind providence that he was not in the old minelaying "U73." For had he been, he too, would have been in Davy Jones's locker, along with the many 1910 cadet classmates.

Between the coast of Italy and the northern extremity of Corfu, he discovered a steel net which had been placed just under the water, so surface craft could pass over it, but down so deep that submarines could barely escape its meshes which extended into the sea almost two hundred feet. Patrol vessels were so thick that they were scarcely able to use their periscope at all. Martin held his U-boat near the coast, so that he could slip through the opening which he thought might be near by. Diving to a hundred and ninety feet, with patrol ships sailing overhead and dropping their depth charges, he managed to worm his way through the net opening and on to safety.

His operation orders read, "Lay a minefield off Marseilles; destroy commerce along the French coast," which he proceeded to carry out with dexterity.

Off Malta when his periscope was upped, he sighted a convoy of about twenty ships, and managed to drive a torpedo into one of them to the tune of the phonograph , playing, *"Deutschland, Deutschland uber alles!"* He exulted too early in this game of death, for at a hundred and sixty feet under the surface he felt the shock of depth charges.

Going down another thirty feet by the use of hand gear to avoid all unnecessary noise, two more charges were thrown at him, but on sailing for a mile or so northward, when his periscope was upped again, he found the sea calm and the ships out of range.

Martin learned during his "U151" days that the Allies had mastered many new submarine hunting tricks, and numerous had been his hairsbreadth escapes. Nor was he to miss these on his own U-boat. Just before noon of that day, he relieved the navigating officer long enough for him to shoot his noon sight, and as he scanned the horizon, there against the sun, high in the sky, was a black spot.

He barely screamed the command, "Crash dive! a plane!" before the plane had gotten his range. While at a depth of only about forty feet the crash of an aft explosion was followed by one over the conning tower, which knocked him from his feet and threw him against the sub's side. The pistol trigger whizzed into the control room nearly striking him, to be followed by a three-inch stream of water. Then came a forward crash.

It seemed the "UC67's" end was at hand—and Niemoeller's as well. A leak was reported from the engine room in the hatchway. The conning tower

leak was being plugged as fast as possible, while
Martin took a quick look at his charts. He discovered he was off Malta, and if necessary could go
down to two hundred feet and lie on the bottom
while repairs were being carried out.

This slightly relieved his failing spirits. Added to
the then-present difficulties a lead-in pipe developed
a leaky gland and filled one compartment with water.
When Martin later gave the "Up periscope!" command, the mechanism was jammed.

"Up spare periscope!" he countered, and when it
topped the surface, everything was pitch dark. It
also had been smashed by the explosion. "We now
feel really uneasy," he says, "a submarine without
a periscope ceases to be a submarine and is merely
a blind cripple."

When night came on, Martin surfaced the "UC67"
and went over it carefully to discover the real
damages, which were many and serious indeed. His
No. 1 torpedo tube was crushed like a "child's rubber
ball." The conning tower was a scramble, along with
an assortment of other disqualifying jolts, jars and
jams.

This was the blow that really struck Martin below
his mental belt. It was obvious that they must make
for port, and difficult indeed he knew that homeward journey to be. So they turned home feeling
that things might have turned out "differently *if* . . .
But who can fill in that 'if?'—We are alive and
kicking . . ."

At the Straits of Otranto, having timed his arrival
so that it would not be necessary to use his periscope
by day, he crossed the first line of patrol boats safely,
and when night hove on, they surfaced, and three

officers, including the captain, peered into the darkness. Martin realized that a mistake just at that time would have been fatal. For the sub was dumb and very blind indeed.

Nearing the sub-catching net, a motor boat forced them to submerge to a depth of a hundred and ninety feet, and at a speed of three knots, he tried to outdistance the surface vessels which loosed a barrage of depth charges.

Nor was there any question of the submarine's coming up, "for we are both blind and deaf." From noon onward oxygen was released, and while sluggish-minded officers should have long before turned in for the night's rest, they could not. Nor was Martin able to retire, his mind awhirl with plans and tricks and techniques of avoiding the fateful death-bomb, which at any moment he expected.

In the midst of this, Martin as all men in danger's most critical hours turned his thoughts God-ward. He asked himself: *Is there peace anywhere?* Will peace come, or shall we spend year after year at sea without rest or respite? These and other soul-challenging questions led him to the eternal issue: *life, the universe and God.* "These questions are not prompted by curiosity . . . they force themselves upon us. All we know is that we have not found the answer to them."

This is a different Martin at twenty-six, deep in the sea's belly, from Martin at forty-six whose faith while in the concentration camp is sky-high and whose redemption song rings with an "I know" assurance. Between the two Martins—the sea-belly sailor and the mouthpiece of God—there were to come many life-altering experiences through which he should be tried as by spiritual fire.

Limping back to the Pola dockyard for a thorough checking, he decided while the submarine was being repaired that he would go to Berlin, "not for the purpose of looking up the admiralty but to obtain the promised yes from the girl I love."

Nor was that *yes* long in coming, for he stayed in Berlin only twenty-four hours and hastened to Elberfeld where his engagement was formally announced. The future at that time looked dark and uncertain to him, and above all, fate-dimmed. He had made one valuable discovery which was to keep his soul's periscope upped during the trying years that were to come: *Life is not what we know and plan for, but what we believe and dare!*

This was Martin Niemoeller when the cocksureness had been knocked out of him by dozens of exploding depth charges. He was being tutored by the inexorable hand of difficulties. His soul madness was shaped to a nobler destiny by problematic maneuvers in the realm of the spiritual and the physical as well.

By August the "UC67" was ready for action, and Martin's soul, well-sobered by the knowledge that the war was nearing its end—an end tragic in its implications for his nation—faced the final test before he broke with his old navy past. His new orders read: *Destroy commerce.* But in the midst of this destruction the old exuberance at amidship hits, a ship wallowing in the death throes, flames shooting sky-high from exploding ammunition was lacking. He was somber at such sights.

Sinking two steamers from a convoy, one shot
flame three hundred feet into the air, and Martin remarked, "The same dreadful sight!" Previously
this had been a scene in which his mind reveled.
When the escorting ships began salvaging survivors,
Martin's sub did not stick its nose up here and yon
to hinder their lifesaving operations. Not this
rapidly changing Martin's submarine!

"Homeward is the word for us," he says after this
gruesome destruction of life and commerce. Oil
supply was running low and things in general did not
check up to quite the right score in Martin's soul. Off
Sardinia on the morning of September 21, a quick-
witted destroyer captain unloaded a salvo of depth
bombs on Martin's already scarred "UC67," as well
as upon Martin's rapidly altering outlook.

The sea's belly, by the Straits of Otranto, to
Niemoeller became a life-challenging scene. Possibly
Martin had misread the stars as to the direction of
his life's career, and the sea-belly might have been
to him what the whale's belly was to Jonah. Martin
wirelessed his memorable report to the Flotilla, and
suddenly he and Topp, facing life as it really is, began to discuss the drift of their careers when the war
was over. The commander keynoted his own future
by exclaiming, as much to his amazement as to
Topp's disgust, "Then I will be a parson."

The thing was out! It had been festering in his
soul for some time, building as the psychiatrists
would tell us a "life-entangling parson-complex" in
his unconscious mind, finally to burst through to the
spotlight of conscious thought and become a controlling motive in his future life.

As though ashamed of his parson-declaration, Martin added, "It was just a passing thought," and let it go at that.

This was his thirteenth trip through the Straits of Otranto, and Martin, on being reminded of it by Topp, remarked that this "thirteen" superstition was a very devil and one difficult to exorcise.

Superstition or no, five motor boats almost jumped down the "UC67's" hatch, and depth bombs came so fast that it was difficult to keep count of them, to be followed on September 26 by two torpedoes from a hostile submarine! The first one passed before them, while the second was a direct hit. Seconds according to the chronometer of Martin's mind seemed like hours. "Nothing happens." Yet at the very moment Martin saw the torpedo surface long enough to split in half and sink. It was a dud!

A dud! . . . but for Martin's inner soul it was alive with meaning. Torpedo duds are so few and so seldom encountered that to be hit amidship by one and live through it is enough to sober any fire-eating submarine commander's thinking.

By October Niemoeller was certain the war was in its final death throes and that his nation would be the loser. On October 27 a dozen German subs were towed out to sea and sunk by explosive charges. Martin's old "U73," the floating coffin, was among those so graciously interned in the depths of the Mediterranean.

On the homeward trip, when he was delivering his craft to the admiralty for the last time, Niemoeller realized as he passed through the tragical Straits of Otranto, thick with hundreds of German and enemy mines, that it was only a kind Providence which kept

vigil over crippled sub and its soul-weary commander.

"My heart is in my mouth," he exclaims. "God
watches over the brave sailor, but he must steer his
own course. Who steered this one?" From that
moment on a deep-rooted consciousness of a further
mission in life with a new and distinctive meaning
and measure was constantly with Martin. He felt
that God was then directing the helm of his sub as
well as of his soul.

A few days later he was off the coast of Morocco on
November 11, and due to enemy craft was forced to
spend the day at periscope depth. He knew nothing
of the armistice, but sailed on belly-deep in the sea
for his home port of Kiel, arriving on November 30
with ensigns flying.

For Martin a new day was dawning, as well as for
Germany and the world. He had won his spurs, and
in guiding that wet-nosed U-boat through the seas,
God had taken the helm of his soul in hand, and
henceforth the Divine was to play the leading role
in his spiritual pilgrimage.

Chapter IV

FROM U-BOAT TO PULPIT

"Attention facing aft!" said Commander Martin, when the "UC67's" crew had gathered on deck at Kiel. "Lower ensign and pennant."

Thus came to an end Martin's submarine career, for his old U-boat would never again fly the German naval ensign. The Armistice gave her to England, and when he packed the ship's ensign and pennant in his suitcase, he really turned his back upon the only career for which he had prepared himself. He was still in the navy, but his career was at an end.

Likewise Martin was at the frayed terminus of his own life's rope. He had played out the rope of his own thinking until there was no more of it. A new thread of life must now be fabricated for him, and this by a devious path God was preparing.

When his ship's crew left Kiel in the middle of December, he went on leave to his grandparents in Westerkappeln, where he arranged to meet the lady who was to become Frau Niemoeller. He longed to talk to his own father, but since Elberfeld was in the neutral zone, it was temporarily closed to him. His future mother-in-law was deeply stirred by the turn in Germany's fate, and tried to find some comfort from Martin's assurance. But he also faced a dark path into the unknown tomorrows and the ring of his comforting words was hollow.

Since Christmas Martin and his fiancee Else Bremer had been studying Spanish at the Berlitz School of

Languages in order that they might emigrate to Argentina where he had a faint idea of becoming a sheep farmer. The thought had been growing upon him for some time, from which his folk dissuaded him as much as possible. This was, however, the seed of a new life which later was to steer his feet carefully toward the ministry.

His leave ran out on January 26, and he reported to the Kiel inspector-general of submarines for further duty. Five days later he was handed a sealed envelope which contained his orders. On opening it, he discovered that he was to take a dockyard tug and tow two submarines to England in compliance with the armistice terms.

He rushed to Commodore Heinrich's office full of indignation, and said, "Sir, I have received an order which I will not carry out." Inquired the officer, "What is the order?" Niemoeller held it out for him to read, saying, "I have sailed in submarines for three years, fighting against England, sir; I have neither sought nor concluded this armistice. As far as I am concerned, the people who promised our submarines to England can take them over. I will not do it."

The commodore hesitated a moment and then said that he would pass the order to another officer to be carried out. There was no censure, no argument, which Martin could not understand, but later the commodore told Niemoeller that at the time he himself would not have carried out such an order.

When the commodore handed the order to another officer, who in turn objected to carrying it out, the retort was, "You will obey or resign your commission." And he obeyed. Martin, however, did not stay in the navy, being disgusted with the terms of surrender, and was consequently skyhigh as to his own outlook. Through a providence in the early part of 1919, he barely missed an appointment with a Leipzig publishing house, which would have directed his work toward the field of education and not the ministry.

An uncle who lived in the same region as his grandparents wrote him saying that if he wanted to be a sheep farmer there were many available farms in Westphalia and hence no need of his going to the Argentina.

"The scales seemed to drop from my eyes on receiving the letter," he says, and at once preparation was made for him to work for a farmer by name of Wieligmann, more or less as an apprentice or farm-understudy.

Arrangements outlined for his future work, he was married by his father at Elberfeld on Easter Sunday, even though his father-in-law lifted his eyebrows in doubt as to his new occupation. When asked what his marriage prospects were founded on, Martin replied, "On a whole heap of courage."

On May 5 the middle-aged farmer for whom he was to work drove to his grandparents' home where Martin's things, consisting of a bed and chest of clothes, were loaded in the farm wagon.

Martin Niemoeller, who had commanded his own submarine, built a noteworthy career for himself as a specialist in a dangerous field, had now become a full-fledged farmer's helper. He had gone all the way from fame, achievement to an occupation which depended upon brawn and native wit.

"So I plowed furrow after furrow, and before the evening set in the beet field was ready for fertilizing . . . There was plenty of work to be done on the ninety-acre farm . . . woods to be cleared . . . Garden, stable and farmyard all called for work with spade, fork and saw . . . my favorite work was the daily mowing and collecting of green fodder for the cattle; it involved an early morning start with a horse and small wagon to the pastures . . . with the sky lit by the rising sun and the earth shrouded with a thin mist. My German home!"

This is farmer Martin talking, but while he was cutting the fodder, spading in the soft, fertile earth, clearing the woods, he had time for the first instant in his life to think those destiny-propelled thoughts which had been rambling through his subconscious mind for so many years. In the battleground of his mind he torpedoed his way through, as he had done in his old sub, to a glorious conclusion.

His wife meanwhile had secured an appointment with a neighboring farmer that she, too, might become an apprentice, learning the role of a German farmer's wife—preparing butter, caring for milk, feeding the little calves, serving as midwife to sows in the throes of birth pains. Martin was deep in his penetration of nature's secrets of agricultural productivity and was cutting his way through the intricacies of commercial fertilizers and barnyard manure.

He had gone all the way, and a farmer he would become. As the rains washed sky and earth clean, so this process of losing himself in farm problems was cleaning the clouds from his own brain; washing his mind thoroughly; drenching out the thoughts of his own self-sufficiency; and was bringing him step by step nearer the sense that his life and his future depended upon God, in whose hands he was.

Deep in the potato patch in the middle of September, he was lost in the maze of what to do . . . rent a little farm, for indeed his little capital would not buy one. He kept calculating and worrying, debating against the inevitable proposition: for him there was but one possible position—a paid job on a farm. "That was a prospect I could not face."

The potatoes were finally dug, and once finished, Martin seemed to write completion to his quest. On September 17, he started to Kappeln for a heart-to-heart talk with his uncle, when accidentally he ran into Reverend Johann to Settel, "and greeted him."

After leaving the parson and his gracious greeting, it came to him that once he had told Topp he would become a parson. "How was it," he asked himself, "that I had never thought of it since?"

Then it occurred to him wherein the trouble lay. He had as a result of his postwar experiences drifted away from his parents, their religious activities, the glory of the church and its life-altering program—in a spiritual sense. God was as near as his own breath of prayer; yet he had failed to find this source of Divine strength.

He had built a barrier around himself, thus shutting himself from the church, his people and his God. "And now I suddenly knew that the last few months had made a new man of me."

Then the barriers fell from around him; the scales dropped from his spiritual eyes, and he saw the only clear path that led into the mysteries of his own future. He wrote in his diary that night, *"Am going into the church!"* Martin says little about the spiritual implications of that decision, but they were sufficient to start him on the glory road that in the end gave him grace to stand even though it might mean his death before Hitler's axman or firing squad.

The next night he placed his decision before Father Niemoeller in a letter deep with emotion and charged with decisiveness. He shrank from public speaking, from "the idea of having to preach extempore, as a parson," and thought he would like to take up philology, German divinity and religious history.

This was the man who was to become Germany's most popular preacher and whose pulpit address is a challenge to all who hear him! A tongue-tied Moses who was to become his own eloquent Aaron.

He had seen the Gospel of Christ, through hearing the Word preached, remake men and cause weaklings to become strong and free in the Lord. "This teaching was one I took with me from the home of my childhood days, and I had clung to it through all the vicissitudes of life." Thinking thus, he decided that he could best serve his fellow men as a minister of the Master, and could do more for people in their present tragic postwar lives by devoting himself to religious work than by self-seclusion in a pigsty.

The next Monday afternoon in the pigsty he told his decision to farmer Wieligmann, who gladly released him from his term of services. But those potatoes Martin loved, and since a few of them huddled themselves in Mother Earth's bosom, he wanted to stay on until the last little fellow had been bedded down in the good farmer's bin.

In a pouring rain the next afternoon he went to see the Kappeln preacher, Johann to Settel, whose kind greeting had turned his preacher-gropings into a full-fledged decision to become a parson. And the minister promised to teach him the elements of Hebrew, necessary for theological matriculation.

The last little potato (which Martin had deeply learned to love in his sub days when for weeks the crew was out of them) had been slipped into its bin-bed on October 2, and on the fourth (how Martin remembered and counted those days!) the last load of green fodder had been cut. The rain had fallen all day on the farm in gentle drippings, and the evening was clear and pleasant when "I took my leave and started out for my new goal."

Having matriculated at Munster for his theological course, he found it possible to live with his grand-parents for the first six months of his student days. He was hard set to master the elements of Hebrew, which was a requirement of his course. Having taxed his brain by learning hundreds of Spanish words, he found the new Hebrew words an added burden, but by the aid of his wife he carried on, and prepared for the examination by the end of December, 1919.

Luckily Pastor Kaehler of Munster had an apart-ment to let in the rectory and Martin and his wife packed their meager belongings and moved them by farmer's cart on December 15. He had spent eight days chopping his winter's supply of wood, while the Frau had preserved provisions in jars and glasses.

Since his money was limited it was necessary for them to practice the most careful economies.

He says of his examination before the seminary's faculty, "The unpacking of the spiritual baggage on the following day turned out well, but the furniture van took longer to clear than we had anticipated."

After the twenty-seventh of November when he received the official notification that his release from the navy was final, he gave up looking back on his naval career "and ceased wondering whether I should turn about." He had placed his hands to the Gospel plow, he reminded himself, and no man, looking back, "is fit for the kingdom." And now matriculation and examination completed, he was more certain that this was his life.

The navy, however, did a service which made it possible for him to finish his theological course by granting a small pension for his term of activity. At the time he thought little of this gratuity, but later when his capital funds were exhausted, this bridged the gap between hunger and at least a morsel of food for himself and Frau Else.

His courses of study for the 1920 term consisted of "The History of the Church During the Reformation," dogma, ecclesiastical history, Westphalian church history, and two courses in the Old and New Testaments. "Bible study," he adds, "was and still is the focus of my whole course of learning."

When his financial worries became the most bothersome, he was offered a position as manager of a Rhenish factory. But in advising with his wife, he felt that God had opened a door into the ministry, and indicated that he was to step into it; so he turned down the tempting offer. All he could say of the decision was that they never regretted it.

His studies during the first year were interrupted by local disturbances due to the political revolution going on in the nation at the time, and the theolog saw action with the Academic Defense Corps. While he was serving with his troops, he received a telephone call on Good Friday, and was elated when his mother announced, "You have a little daughter; she is fair and has blue eyes." Inquiring about his Else, he was told the mother was doing very well.

This little Brigitte was the first of seven children God gave to Martin and Else, the last having been born shortly after the Gestapo threw its clutches upon him and imprisoned this man of destiny.

When the spring term closed, Martin and his family spent the long vacation, as they did the subsequent ones, with his father's family in Elberfeld. Nor could his mind remain inactive during this time, for he devoted the mornings to studying the Psalms and the Gospels, chinking in his spare moments by reading deep theological tomes that he might lay a worthy foundation upon which his new career as Christ's ambassador was to be built.

The university terms followed in rotation and Martin kept close to his studies, taking time however to meet the various evangelical pastors in Munster. Here he met the bishop of Westphalia, Dr. Zoellner, who later was to give him his first church employment. The contact with Pastor Kaehler was of such a happy nature that when he was ready for his curacy, he spent the year serving in the pastor's Munster parish.

He had dreamed of attending another university instead of Munster, but finances, having beached him, took the air out of this inflated blimp of an idea. So it must be Munster until graduation.

God's hand directed Niemoeller in these student years, and especially during August, 1921, when he had gotten down to the very bottom of his financial barrel. He received an offer from Berlin to take a ship to the Mediterranean for a couple of months. The boat's cargo consisted of munitions for Turkish delivery, and though he would have been well recompensed for his services, he did not relish the idea because the British were controlling the Dardanelles and the Bosphorus.

Turning down the position, he learned later that the ship had been seized and the crew held prisoners for considerable time. Had he been along, this imprisonment would have seriously interfered with his theological studies.

During his fifth term, following the vacation season, he attended the homiletic seminary of the university, where each student was expected to preach a sermon. Martin's appointment to deliver his first message came on December 15, 1921, and the text given him by the seminary was, "My soul doth magnify the Lord."

When he arose to speak before the professor and a dozen or so theological students, he made a good start but his mind seemed to freeze, and he found it necessary to consult his notes. As this occurred again in a few moments, he seemed to have become accustomed to the thought of doing the sermon indifferently and proceeded to finish the message.

Though the criticisms were not unfavorable, he
returned home that night in a state of defeat, feeling
as though the sub of his ministerial career had been
struck by a depth bomb.

Not to be outdone, he telephoned his father for
permission to repeat the sermon in his church the
following morning. This time the congregation
listened intently, which in turn gave the wings of
inspiration to Martin's fear-tipped words, and he
finished with a sense of having done well his Master's
bidding. That Sunday morning in Father Niemoeller's Elberfeld pulpit was the turning point in the
young parson's preaching career.

"Since that fourth Sunday in Advent," he tells us,
"my only preaching worry has been whether what I
tell the congregation in the name of God is really
delivered in His name and inspired by Him."

During this fifth term he joined the academic
church choir, which did much to renew acquaintance with sacred music, and the fellowship with the
other singers added a homey touch to his seminary
work. On Easter he delivered his second sermon
before his father's congregation.

In his sixth and final term, he had no regular lec-
tures to attend, though his work was heavy and
miscellaneous as he prepared for his final examinations in the subjects he had taken. This did not
bother him greatly for he had always done more or
less instructional work as an officer. During this
period he also assumed part-time leadership of the
children's services in the Munster parish, of which
later he was to have sole charge for more than a year.
At the seminary he assisted with Bible classes as well.
This gave him a broadening contact with parish and

ministerial problems, which when his own ministerial days should begin was a valuable asset in his
work.

He launched 1922 under a serious financial handi-
cap, and when February's blustery days slipped toward their close, he tried to sell the only object of
value he possessed—an old Luther Bible of 1545-46,
which had come from Hans Lufft's press in Witten-
burg. "Thank God," he writes, "we were unable to
find a buyer . . ." Help in due time arrived through
the aid of a brother-in-law who was appointed as a
doctor in a Gottingen clinic for nervous disorders.

The year 1922 was marked with blessing and bane:
blessing in the form of his first son's birth on July
16, and the bane, constant financial worry. The son
he named for a submarine commander friend, a war
casualty, and prayed that little Hans Jochen "would
grow up to be as straight and fine a German as was
this submarine commander." Nor was that prayer
to be unanswered, for Hans since his father's imprisonment has declared that he, with his two
younger brothers, will follow Martin into the
ministry.

He did not wait for the old wolf of poverty to run
love and happiness out the door, but he obtained
employment as a platelayer on the railroad, a common section-hand job. In laying plate he did it with
the same glory and vigor with which he once sent
death-propelling torpedoes into enemy ships. In his
annals he does not detour this difficulty, saying, "The
employment proved most opportune and we used my
pay to purchase stores for the winter."

Working at day labor, he still found time in the
evening to prepare for his examinations. He was

assigned two subjects for his theses: "Was Paul a Witness of Jesus Christ?" and "The Mysticism of Master Eckart and of Bernhard of Clairvaux."

Later he transferred to the railway station accountants' office, which provided living money as well as furnished him with necessary time for his university requirements. His scholastic work proceeded so well that his theses were completed by the middle of December, 1922, which allowed him a month for his written sermon and catechism study, which he finished by January 12, 1923. The last hurdle, his final college examinations, was passed by April 23, which he characterized as "an important stage toward my goal."

Rethinking those days when he "lived from hand to mouth," he looked upon them as furnishing a definite contribution to the spiritual preparation for his vocation of priest and pastor. "I discovered and still know what it feels like to have no fixed means of existence and sustenance, and I see something of special providences in that phase of my life"— special dispensations from God which enabled him to reach his goal.

In May he began his curacy under Dr. Kaehler, which became his initiation into practical Christian work. Until now he had been only a religious theorist, but he must master the needed lessons of turning theory into experience—interpreting books in terms of life. He conducted Bible classes for confirmation twice a week. During one evening each week he held a study-seminar with the workers who helped with the children's services, which he led each Sunday. Added to these burdens was visitation of the sick and aged in the parish.

Each week Rector Kaehler spent several hours with Martin discussing parish duties and church problems. The appointment of the rector as bishop at Settin cut short those valuable sessions in religious practics. Martin wished they might have been of a longer duration.

There were also two places where he preached, "which were neither churches or halls with pulpits." One was at the prisoners' camp on Munster's outskirts, and the other was in the living room of the station master at Telgte, a small place which edged Munster, famed in the Catholic world as the scene of religious pilgrimages. His first love, he affirms years later, "belongs to both these congregations."

His curacy possessed for him many obstacles, for at the end of July when the Kaehlers left Munster, though they were permitted to live in the rectory, still they had nothing but rice stored in a large tin case, "which served to hold my full-dress uniform in the good old days."

They needed money for milk and butter and vegetables, for those growing youngsters must be properly fed. Frau Else set her deft fingers at the task of picking the "gold lace off all my old uniforms" which they had piously preserved. A jeweler melted the gold and bought it for enough money to sustain them for a couple of days. Next went the chronometer from his "U151" days, the proceeds of which enabled them to live for two weeks.

God had not forgotten them, for on August 18, between eight and nine in the evening, the doorbell rang, and Martin faced Mr. Paul, his friend from the accountants' office at the railway station, who had come with an offer of a temporary position. This gave him enough time for his curate duties, and for his second theological or professional examination.

In the midst of those "terrible times," as Martin terms them, when inflation raged and expenses were mountain-high, the thirty-one-year-old preacher-to-be started home one evening having hit a new low in despondency. It seemed that he must find paying employment, but all avenues were closed. Nor was he ready for a parish—and if ready, none was available.

On reaching home in this state, he started to unburden his heart to Else, whose strong faith had been a sustaining arm upon which to lean, when she said, "By the way, the bishop sent a message asking you to come and see him after supper." Divine aid was at hand, no farther away than Bishop Zoellner's.

Weeks earlier the bishop had asked the theolog whether after he had completed his curate's year he would care to join the Inland Mission staff. That evening when Martin saw him the question came once more. The fledgling parson did not debate the issue, for he could not afford to turn down even this type of religious work, though he had hoped for a country parish.

He had learned that God's ways did not always follow the dim outline which he had blazed in his own thinking. Looking firmly at the good bishop, he said, "I regard this offer as from the hand of God and will accept it."

The following day the board of the Westphalian Inland Mission met and appointed Niemoeller as manager for Westphalia, with duties to begin on December 1, 1923. This gave Martin two weeks in which to complete his examination theses and to clear all items prerequisite to ordination.

When he told his wife the nature of his new duties, neither of them were happy at the prospect, for they had hoped for a peaceful pastorate where they might get close to the needs of their people. This position was the opposite, for it entailed conferences, business meetings, journeys and many addresses and speeches, sessions with the clergy and state and city officials, as well as organizational and financial oversight and management.

The main issue at the time consisted of coordinating the various independent Protestant, especially Lutheran, charitable organizations in the several cities and districts, and bringing them under the leadership of the church's special societies and committees for youth and charity. The State was rapidly absorbing such charitable activities, founded and sustained by the church, into the governmental welfare administration. This, of course, would have made them political and social groups, rather than religious bodies and activities.

The Inland Mission of the Westphalian province directed and controlled several hundred such institutions and groups. It was Niemoeller's duty to supervise these and coordinate their several polities under church leadership. This required weeks of travel, addressing diocesan assemblies and clergy groups, as well as conferences with state and provincial officials. Later Martin was nominated to fill Dr. Kaehler's vacancy on the Consistory Board, which broadened his activities but caused him to confess he thought he should have studied economics rather than theology.

He contented himself with conducting the Munster children's services, and preaching in the church once a fortnight. He laments, "But I had no parish, neither had I any time to gather a circle of young people in my house."

In May of 1924 he completed his final professional examination, which marked the end of his official tests, and brought to a successful termination his four years of apprenticeship. Consequently, on June 29 he was ordained with two other young preachers in the Munster Church of the Redeemer. The service was conducted by the Right Reverend Dr. Simon, with Father Niemoeller assisting.

As it proceeded, Martin's mind was filled with this question: *Am I now a complete and qualified man?* It was a serious occasion, and as the sacred rite unfolded, a ceremony filled with gracious dignity and blessed with the sireship of Martin Luther, Niemoeller's heart warmed to the glowing glory of the charges.

Being the oldest of the ordination candidates, it fell to Martin to deliver the sermon, preaching from the words, "Not as though I had already attained, either were already perfect: but I follow after, if that I may apprehend that for which also I am apprehended of Christ Jesus" (Phil. 3:12).

To seal his spiritual attainment of an ordained minister's status, Martin went to the attic apartment which had been the wrestling place with want and privation during his student days, and arranged his desk for a baptismal altar. He placed thereon the crucifix, the candlesticks and the font. The window to the rear of this altar was draped with the ensign of the submarine he commanded, the "UC67," and which it had flown when he entered Kiel on November 29, 1918.

And in that setting he baptized their youngest son Heinz Herman, using for the text the words, "Oh give thanks unto the Lord for he is good; for his mercy endureth forever!"

The journey from submarine to pulpit had come to an end, and Martin's service for God and country, in his new profession, was dawning.

After Martin had been imprisoned in a Hitler concentration camp, he is reported to have said that while he was fighting as a naval officer in the World War he was motivated by a feeling that all the fighting was for something unworthy and without meaning in the timeless glow of eternity.

This meaning he found in his call to proclaim God's Word as a servant of the Church. The deeper he delved into the Bible the more majestic its truths became to his soul. It was upon this Word that he laid the foundation for his successful pastorate to come and which now in his prison cell sustains him with its unfailing strength.

He was to build a faith which in time of trial would cry out, "God is my Fuehrer." This was sufficient for him, and he determined to found his life-labor upon the Divine program as outlined in the Bible.

Chapter V

"GOD IS MY FUEHRER!"

Martin by this time had thoroughly freed his soul from all naval entanglements; and the scars the war had left on his mind were erased by the full knowledge that his feet at last had found what for him was the king's highway. He who had dreamed of helping to conquer the world was now thoroughly conquered by the noble idea of winning the world to his Master.

As he had once fired his torpedoes for victory, he now was to turn loose all the guns of his soul in the Christian battle. He had been thoroughly fitted by nature and training for command. By experience he had come through all the necessary stages of personality equipment whereby he might marshal men, an ability which was soon to force him to the higher rungs in his new ministerial career.

He and Frau Else had dreamed of a quiet retreat in some perfect pastoral scene where he might delve thoroughly into the Bible, perfect his public address and come to grips with the seedy problems of hungry-hearted postwar Germans. But God was to season him in public without the quiet pastoral retreat. Martin's soul called for action, and Martin's ability required the clash of mental guns against State officials who were gradually trying to break the Church's long arm of charitable institutions. His new position with the Westphalian Mission proved the seasoning arena for his battle with Hitler.

74

Here he met public officials on their own ground and stood as the defender of the Church. He learned how to outwit their keenest schemers as he once was able to dodge England's most brilliant destroyer commanders. His submarine strategy now became Christian tactics. He had something for which to fight that was worthy of all his abilities—and this even in face of an eternal scale of values.

Niemoeller threw himself into his new work with a will to win; and win he did. He wrote Christian history in those early years as before he had inscribed a brilliant page in submarine warfare. The part of his new work, which at first he faced with dread, became his most loved labors. He traveled extensively throughout the province, and his constant speaking in conferences and before clerical groups polished his ability to handle group situations until he became one of the outstanding Christian strategists.

This art was so pronounced in his work that later, as leader of the new Confessional Church to which he gave birth, his very "no" was sufficient to block an action with the clergy who followed him. Often the nod of his head was sufficient sanction to carry a motion or write a most scathing plank into a denunciatory manifesto. This quality was brewed in the crucible of his Mission endeavors.

So after all the Divine Destiny had shaped his life, rough-hew it as he might. For Martin Niemoeller there was never to be the quiet of a pastoral scene. Others might have this honor, but not he. Father Niemoeller in his Elberfeld parish lived the life of a noble and dearly beloved parson of which his famous son dreamed but was not to attain. And even when the aged man became pastor emeritus, the love of his people was sufficient to keep him busy to the end. This was what Martin wanted, but the divine path thrust him into the spotlight of the nation's bustle.

Those were seasoning years, from 1924 until 1931, consisting of travel, public conferences, addresses before magnificent congregations, meeting church and national situations, until Niemoeller's growing fame drew him toward one of the nation's most brilliant and important congregations. His popularity as the U-boat preacher turned the eyes of leaders upon him.

During this time postwar Germany was in the throes of revolution, even dissolution. The old had passed away; a republic had been promulgated with the famed war general Von Hindenberg at the fore. Gradually the cementing bonds within the populace began to break away. The nation was looking for a man with a message and a program which hinted at an even more brilliantly hued future. And that man was a house painter with a little mustache.

The same thing that gave Hitler his opportunity, the concreteness of his program and message, was to throw Martin into the seething maelstrom of Church circles. He had a dynamic message for men in trouble. It was the manifesto of Martin Luther, of the glorious all-encompassing power of the Gospel to meet human needs. Niemoeller never deviated in his Christian pronouncements. His sermons never delved into the speculative; the pen that wrote his Sunday messages was never dipped into criticism, doubt and religious perfidy that sapped the Divine from the Bible—a popular practice in prewar seminary and pulpit. Not Martin's. He preached, he wrote, he heralded but one way out—the Christian path of redemption through Christ's magnificent power.

This was Niemoeller's credo. Not once in his published sermons does he detour from it. American visitors who heard him preach, as Professor Alex Craig, a West Coast linguist, say that his messages were touched with the divine simplicity of the old Gospel.

This drew men to Martin's ministry and opened a broadened field for his services. He knew the Christian path to the heights and men were willing to listen when he guided them. As Hitler rose to power by offering a positive program for social and economic betterment, which in the end made him the nation's chief contender for the title of god, so Martin's Christian way through cast the spotlight of public hero-worship upon him.

Slowly and gradually these two achieved fame and leadership, each with a positive program for life betterment: one the Gospel and the other Hitlerism, Nazism, dubbed National Socialism. Both grew from seedlings into trees that shaded all of Germany's life—one in the sphere of Evangelical faith and the other in the socio-civil order. It was inevitable that the two should meet and in the end clash, for they were diametrically opposed one to the other.

At first Martin Niemoeller looked favorably upon Hitler's economic panacea. He was faithful to Hitler's program from 1924 until his assumption of power in 1933.

In 1931 Niemoeller became the pastor of the Dahlem parish, which consisted of two churches: Jesus Christus Kirche and St. Anne's, over which three pastors presided—Martin and his two assistants. Dahlem is a wealthy and important residential suburb or district of Berlin, where many famous scholars, doctors and retired naval officers, along with leading political figures, live. The Church of Jesus Christ's membership at the time was the most influential of any that was favorable to Hitler.

This is housed in a graystone edifice, resembling a political hall rather than a house of God, and its six hundred seats Niemoeller packed each Sunday with storm-troopers, bankers, lawyers, scholars and their families who went through the Lutheran rites and listened intently to his evangelical sermons.

On assuming this pastorate he did not deviate from his fiery sermons on Biblical themes; rather he intensified them. His public messages gave little attention to the political situation, dealing rather with the problems of the soul as they are outlined in God's Word. During those early years in Dahlem he gave the Nazi salute and was on friendly terms with many of Hitler's early supporters and assistants.

In January, 1931, Hitler called several leading Protestant clergymen to meet with him at the Hotel Kaiserhof, Berlin, for a conference on religious issues. Martin was among the group and Hitler recognized him. When Niemoeller told the Austrian house painter he was no longer an officer in the navy, but was serving in a humble manner as a Christian pastor, Hitler pointed out the great need of Germany for men like Herr Kapitan who dared go straight from U-boat to the pulpit.

Hitler is reported to have told the preachers that he also was working for the moral rebuilding of the nation, which since the war had slithered to the slough of defeat and despondency. He flung before them the challenge which the church must face in crushing atheism and re-establishing belief.

In Niemoeller's public work immediately follow-ing this conference, he felt that the program as then outlined was for the Church's as well as the State's benefit and for the time being he was willing to trail along in the Hitler camp.

There was much for Martin to do in his wealthy and flourishing parish of ten thousand members, and he threw himself into this work with the vigor which marked his submarine days. During the next fifteen months he went about his time-consuming and energy-demanding duties as the spiritual leader of his people. He not only pastored his own parish but began to assume a position of service to a grow-ing group among Berlin's four million inhabitants.

They made a constantly enlarging demand upon his time for weddings, funerals and christenings; the capital's clergy called for Martin's strong hand upon the helm of their church functionings. His voice was dominant in conference with his fellow pastors. Dur-ing this period he gave little attention to Hitler's rise to power. Pastor Niemoeller knew that it would not be long until Hitler would seize the reins of govern-ment.

As pastor, however, he was more concerned with the spiritual well-being of his flock than with move-ments among the National Socialists. Hence his con-tacts with these groups were infrequent at this time. By the spring of 1932 other pastors were looking with dread upon Hitler's growing importance in the nation, and a federated group of preachers asked

Pastor Niemoeller to discover the real meaning of Hitler's national program.

There were enlarging signs that this program was not as Hitler had seemingly outlined it earlier. Storm troopers had begun an inexorable line of murders. The Hitler Youth were no longer walking the Christian way. The Nazi propaganda sheets were flaunting an anti-church sentiment. The Berlin pastors, among whom Niemoeller stood as leader, wanted to know the meaning of these activities.

The pastor went away from his second conference with Hitler, who had also called in Goering and other high Nazi officials, sensing all was not well with the national schedule as programmed by Hitler still he could not lay his finger upon the disturbing elements. It was at this meeting that Hitler gave the preacher his solemn word of honor!

Martin's pulpit declarations had much to say about the faith which Martin Luther had so ably defended even at the risk of his life. And in the face of Nazi atrocities which were becoming more dastardly, he urged his people to remain calm in their religious beliefs. He saw the rapid decline in religion, and heard the Nazis' fiery speeches against the church which were directed at inflaming the masses.

Martin was particularly disturbed over the fact that notary publics for a fee of two marks would receipt exemptions from church membership. Since these were looked upon as being legally valid, there was an alarming decrease in church attendance. With this a tide of moral laxity swept the nation, and marriages without the Church's blessings were becoming a frequent occurrence.

The pastor saw many couples who dispensed with the marriage ceremony, since the sacred rite had become a mere civil contract, and simply lived together in illegal and adulterous union.

Church baptisms and confirmations became fewer and fewer as parents were engrossed with Hitlerism. Church offerings fell off, and the lack of funds placed on a precarious foundation charitable tasks which the Church had assumed.

It was clear to Niemoeller and other pastors of the Evangelical Church that the very existence of organized religion depended upon Hitler's promised restoration of a close connection between State and Church. Hence the fighting pastor trailed along in the Hitler camp until it became evident those promises were to be classed as fabrications only, to enmesh the faithful in his web of dawning tyranny.

Niemoeller's sermon on January 30, 1933 revealed that he greeted Hitler's assumption of office with a heart full of thanks. On March 21, in Hitler's address to the Reichstag, he said, "The National Socialist government thinks the two Christian churches are the most important elements for the preservation of our national individuality . . . Their rights shall not be touched."

This caused Niemoeller to rejoice before his congregation that at last the future for the Church looked brighter than previously. However by the time of the election on May 27 of the new bishop for the entire German church, it was evident that this rejoicing was premature. The Evangelical group acting for the twenty-eight provincial churches which made up the Lutheran and Reformed organizations had elected their own candidate as national bishop.

Dr. Freidrich von Bodelschwingh, the new bishop, was not acceptable to Hitler and the Nazi authorities, and so a former army chaplain and close friend of Hitler, Ludwig Muller, became the party candidate. When the election arrived, all channels of publicity were controlled by the Nazis, and Hitler himself came forward to demand Muller's election as the new Reichsbishop. This meant that at last the State through Muller was in supreme control of the Church and there was no more religious freedom.

Such sentiment received official expression when at the first national meeting of the German Christians, as Hitler's new religious group was called, Dr. Werner proclaimed that whatever Hitler orders, the Church must perform.

By degrees this new German or positive religion, in distinction to "negative" religion, which the Lutheran Church proclaimed, spread its tentacles through the cultural life of the nation. It demanded that all Jews be eliminated from church membership and be purged; that all small Evangelical churches be formed into a union under Muller's control. This Nazi religion, known as the German Christians, spread throughout the nation, and was presided over by a German god, in contradistinction to the Christian God, and Hitler was the earthly envoy and fuehrer of the national deity.

Rosenberg, later becoming head of German *kultur,* expressed the essence of the new positive religion, saying, "A German church will gradually represent the Fire Spirit, the Hero in the highest sense, in place of the Crucified One." God was to be positioned in the new regime, as Henry Smith Leiper expresses it, if he too would "Heil Hitler!"

Niemoeller was quick to catch the connotation, and he saw that the Christian pastors had been "sold down the river" by the Hitler program. In his parish meetings, held in the week time, he gave vent to the sentiment that he had been betrayed by a false promise, and showed disappointment that he had given Hitler his support—a support inspired by deliberately false pretenses.

Muller was not long in giving expression to the new order in the religious sphere. In a pamphlet issued in July, 1933, it was said, "He who does not vote for the German Christian list is our enemy. He who is our enemy is the enemy of the state. The enemy of the state will be put on the black list and find himself in a concentration camp." Exactly what Martin did.

In the actual elections early in the summer Niemoeller's congregation gave the German Christian candidates only a bare minority support, for the famous parish was influenced by their pastor's sentiments. A break with Hitler was inevitable.

Niemoeller represented a force which Hitler hated, and which, before he had gained complete control of all national life, he must crush. Already the Old Testament had been scrapped, and the Jewish blood in Jesus made him unacceptable to the new German religious front, unless he became a Nordic Christ.

The fighting pastor reached the limit of endurance before fall and gave vent to his dissatisfaction with a Christianity void of Christ; a Church in which the Storm Troop took the place of Christian freedom; and a religious faith without the Holy Bible in its entirety.

When Niemoeller realized that Hitler's positive religion was plotting the conquest of the entire Evangelical—Lutheran, Reformed, and smaller sects—church by terroristic methods, he contacted likeminded Christian leaders, among whom were Pastor Jacobi, Dr. Kock, Dr. Asmussen and Pastor Muller, for the purpose of forming an emergency league to defend the genuine faith.

The name of this was the Pastor's Emergency League, which at times drew a membership of from three to seven thousand pastors. The resultant group, banding itself loosely into a national organization, became known as the Confessional Church. The name was used to denote the fact that it was founded upon and that its pastors and church members believed and accepted the great Confessions as their dogmatic statement. Niemoeller became the titular head of the group.

The movement was not long in finding expression and attracting adherents throughout the nation. Since Hitler's first objective was to crush all forms of Semitism, the historical sections of the Old Testament were thrown out of German religious literature. The basic attack was thus directly upon the Bible. Hence Niemoeller founded his new religious group upon a defense of the Bible as the unalterable Word of God.

His sermons rang with the evangelical note as founded upon God's Word, which Hitler was trying to erase from the people's minds.

Conditions rapidly came to a head and on November 11, 1933, because Niemoeller and the Confessional Churchmen stood in the path of the Nazi's program of anti-Semitism, Hossenfelder, leader of the Nazi

Christian movement, forced Niemoeller's removal as pastor of the Dahlem parish. This gave birth to a religious furor, second to none, among the influential Dahlem members, who demanded a revocation of the removal order.

Hitler's ears were to the religious ground and when he heard this rumble, his higher-ups passed the word along that the fuehrer wanted the pastor reinstated, which was duly done on the following day.

This was the fighting parson's first direct tilt with the Hitler regime, but it was not to be his last. The breach between the defense bloc, crystallized in the Confessional Church, and German Christian movement became wider, until the hour should come when Germany was not large enough to hold both Hitler in the saddle and Niemoeller free in his pulpit.

Hitler must bide his time until he was strong enough to destroy the parson entirely or clip his wings by arresting him. This was three years away, but steadily the Gestapo dogged the pastor's heels until the hour of his arrest arrived. With this arrest based upon the direct command of the "No. 1 bad boy of Nazism," Hitler has never become sufficiently strong, sufficiently dominant in the nation to defy the Confessional Church, sired by the U-boat preacher, and order his death on the axman's block or before the firing squad.

Such an act would further alienate more than one-eighth of the nation's evangelical pastors, including the retired ones, and by far a stronger circle of church members. This has been a price the fuehrer is afraid to pay. To state a conclusion which naturally follows in later chapters, this is why Hitler did

not martyr Martin Niemoeller on arrest and why he
dares only keep him in a concentration camp.

The day after Martin regained his pulpit, Hitler's
German Christians held a national meeting in Berlin,
at which they went the full length in proclaiming the
tenets of their new faith. They repudiated the Old
Testament, wiped from its dogmas the forgiveness of
sins, and blotted out the thought of a suffering Christ.
Matters had progressed so far that the Confessional
Church must either accept the doctrines thus laid
down or face direct assault.

Standing at the fore of this new band of evangelical Christians was the one obstacle Hitler faced
—Martin Niemoeller.

On December 24, 1933, when the Hitler bishop had
sent out a demand that in all German churches a
uniform service be held, with pastors preaching from
the identical text, and singing the same songs,
Niemoeller said, "We refuse to be dragooned into
having a prescribed text." The Pastor's Emergency
League would not thus set up a service which re-
sembled "a military drill."

When 1934 dawned Niemoeller saw that his one
redress in the growing storm was to appeal directly
to Hitler, who might assist in solving some of the
problems facing the Confessional group. Consequently he met the fuehrer early in January. The
conference was not satisfactory to the pastor, for at
this time Hitler's true nature was evidenced.

On Sunday, January 7, following his meeting with
Hitler, Niemoeller said from his pulpit, "We refuse
to be muzzled." That statement, though short, carried a tremendous meaning, for the pastor had been

threatened with death, and soon the first attempt against his life was to occur.

During the day he spoke at the Church of St. Paul to a thousand youth, ranging in ages from fourteen to twenty, who were members of the German Bible Circle. When Martin thought of Hitler's demand that he be considered the supreme authority in life and morals for the nation, he declared, "God is my Fuehrer!" It was upon this sentence that the fighting parson was to build his future career.

"It seems as if God has meant death in the German Church," he told the youth gathering. "There is a darkness all around us. The church is the ship of safety, but today it appears that this ship is in deadly peril. We must be more obedient to God than to man."

Secret police rushed into the meeting and broke it up. While Niemoeller stood at attention, the youth leaders were arrested, and the youth processional was stopped upon Hitler's authority. The pastor now stood face to face with the full fledged meaning of Nazism, which at its heart is Hitler. Though Hitler was demanding that Christian dogma be adjusted to the trends of the age, Niemoeller knew that he for one looked upon Christian faith as being unalterable. Whatever the demands or threats of Hitler, the Dahlem pastor bowed rather to God than to man.

Martin recognized that Hitler's words held the authority of life or death over him and his people, and however tremendous the threats, in the preacher's soul there was no tendency to "obey man rather than God." Hitler's public declarations were that he was superior to Christ the Jew, more powerful than

He, yet to the Dahlem leader God alone was Fuehrer.

He had challenged Hitler's authority with those words—*God is my Fuehrer!*—and he knew there would be no satisfaction in the Nazi camp until his arrest. Faced now by the hardest struggle of his life, Niemoeller, who had defied death bombs, determined never to surrender.

It was a duel to death and he was as willing to die for Christ as he had been to lay down his life deep in the sea's belly for his nation. Seeing the issue clearly, Martin vowed in his soul that his pulpit should ring with the plain declarations of the Word as God's divine and infallible Voice for his day.

Chapter VI

DEFYING DEATH

NIEMOELLER had been told that he must die, and now all the preacher had to do was to wait until the fuehrer had the courage to carry out the threat. While waiting for this, he was not inactive. Had he been a less God-charged man, he would have retreated. But in the moral backbone of this fighter there was not an ounce of retreat from a given position, whether in the pulpit or in a submarine. Since his arrest time and again it has been rumored in Germany and outside that if Niemoeller would promise not to use his pulpit to fight the Nazi religious regime, he could be freed.

Niemoeller knows this even at present, and he knew long before the Gestapo dared arrest him that he could avoid the inevitable clash with Hitler through laying down his religious arms, ceasing his battle for God's Word and the Confessional Church's beliefs. But with his hands to the Gospel plow—a reference which vividly shocked his first hesitancy after the call to preach—he would not default his worthiness for the Kingdom by turning back. Onward he was propelled as by a mighty motive.

He knew he faced death at any moment, but he who had defied death in a U-boat was not afraid to match swords with it in the pulpit. Two days after his Hitler conference, on January 7, as he stood before his Sunday congregation, he made a statement that twice he had refused to obey orders. "Once when asked to tow submarines to Scapa Flow for the English, I refused the order, and when Bishop Ludwig Muller, Primate of the Reich, ordered me to cease my battling and bring my work into line with his desires, I refused again."

While he made no reference in his Sunday service to his two-day-old tilt with Hitler, he did indirectly strike back at the Nazi machine which was trying to subjugate the Church to its demands. This is characteristic of his Sunday sermons, for even during the last year of his public ministry, in the twenty-eight sermons published, few references to his clashes with the Gestapo and the Nazi regime in the circle of religion are to be found.

In his week-day meetings, in confirmation classes for adults, and assemblies, when hundreds would flock to his parish house to hear him, he was freer to discuss problems of the State and to defy the Gestapo.

Toward the end of January, 1934, he was removed from his church, though his name still appeared on the church register as pastor. This meant that he was technically pastor of the parish, though on enforced "official leave of absence." The suspension, as his previous one, was of short duration. Hitler was testing his strength and the Gestapo were seeing just how far they dared go with Niemoeller and still not alienate a very influential class of citizens in the Reich.

During March, Niemoeller and associated members of the Pastor's Emergency League had the courage to state publicly that "the Nazi system which is gradually wearing down the kingdom of God must be abolished." The Dahlem minister felt something of

Luther's power when he said at Worms, "Here I stand. I cannot do otherwise. God help me."

In early May he still gave and received the Nazi salute wherever necessary or convenient. As a member of the German State, he was loyal to the government, which was his Lutheran heritage; but in matters of religion he felt the State's power could not destroy the demands of conscience as it interpreted the Bible. This was exactly Martin Luther's position. He was conscience-bound in his interpretation, and unless convinced by logic and reason, he was unwilling to give up his faith which had been founded upon God's Word.

Willing to use the Nazi salute, he balked at substituting Rosenberg's German gods for the Christian God, and would not accept artificial barriers in racial distinction. A Jew to him was as good as a German, if they were brothers through Christ's redeeming power. Each entered the Kingdom by the Gate which is Jesus, and once in, there were no distinctions. To this, of course, Muller as Hitler's religious stooge objected, for Hitler must have a scapegoat, which he had found in the Jews.

The religious battle began to tell on his strength. His tall form was marked with a haggard expression. The strictest Prussian officer could find no fault with his attire. His clothes were correctly worn as his hair was always properly groomed. In the pulpit his manner was glorified, and his voice rang loudly and appealingly when charged with strong emotion. He could also bury it low in a whisper with no trace of histrionics. As he then stood before his elite Dahlem congregation he poured out his soul to many leaders of the old order, army officers of the new, storm-troop commanders, captains of industry, bankers and educational leaders.

His battle-keyed personality was thrilled with a message for them in their hour of direst spiritual poverty, and though to deliver it meant facing the fuehrer's wrath, still he would not withhold the tiniest morsel of religious truth from them.

When the death of von Hindenberg, on August 2, 1934, removed the last constraining hand from the old yet the new regime, the German Christian group, led by Muller, held a national synod where the reichsbishop demanded every pastor to sign an oath which committed him to the total leadership of Hitler in both the political as well as the religious realm.

Niemoeller, refusing to be driven into an action against his conscience and the Bible, drew up a pledge which was used by himself and many other ministers in the Confessional group. It received wide circulation and threw Martin into the national spotlight. Newspapers took up the pledge and various foreign news agencies popularized it. Here it is:

"I pledge myself to carry out my office as the servant of the Word, bound to the Holy Scripture and the confessions of the Reformation and the right interpretation of the Holy Scripture alone.

"I pledge myself to sacrifice everything in protesting against any violation of such confession.

"To the best of my capacity I share responsibility with those who are persecuted for such confession.

"Under this obligation I testify that in the employment of the Aryan paragraph within the precincts of the church of Christ a violation of the confession is perpetrated."

The Aryan clause referred to was the Nazi order that all Jews who had affiliated themselves with the Christian church should be excluded from such membership; other racial distinctions were also outlined. This was a clear-cut violation of the Gospel's power to make one all nations and kindreds and climes through the Master's redemption. As such Niemoeller was unwilling that the Confessional pastors submit to this outraging of their religious conscience.

The fighting parson's troubles increased at once. A bomb was thrown into his Dahlem parsonage, which though it damaged the building did not injure any of the family. Three other bombings were to follow without serious demolition of house or fatalities to occupants. Thugs during this time gave him a thorough beating, and doubtless would have killed him, had the high Nazi authorities nodded consent.

The opposition tapped his telephone with a dictaphone whereby a phonographic record was kept of all incoming and outgoing conversations. His pamphlets for the encouragement of the Confessional leaders were seized and destroyed. Once the Nazis rumored that he was to be transferred from his pulpit to the chaplaincy of a submarine.

His organization had assumed such political proportions that the State feared him unless in jail, and to this end all the bishop's efforts were bent. Like truth crushed to earth, the more Niemoeller was persecuted the larger became the group worshiping in the Confessional camp and the stronger his national grip upon the religious life of his people.

Reichsbishop Muller, with Hitler's personal power backing him, was not to be stopped by a mere pledge signed by Niemoeller and his hated crowd of defiant ministers. He issued an order dismissing the pastor from his Dahlem parish and appointed to the post a clergyman who wore the cloth cut by the Nazi crowd.

Such a domineering order as this could but strengthen Martin's moral courage and arouse the fighting ire of his congregation and those who believed in the freedom of religious expression. The news scattered throughout Berlin, dribbled to the very corners of the Reich, crossed the Atlantic, roared around the world. Those who could not attend that Sunday service in Dahlem sent up a volume of prayer for this man who carried the banner which once Martin Luther held aloft.

The fashionable crowds of Dahlem packed the church early, for the city had been buzzing with rumor and was awhirl with dynamite. Long before the hour of service arrived, storm troopers in their Nazi uniforms jammed the aisles. There was no more standing room. Every entrance was massed by storm troopers, for the purpose one would have thought to crowd out the dismissed parson.

At the appointed hour Niemoeller stepped into the pulpit as if nothing had occurred, while the storm troopers blocked the path of the Nazi clergyman who was to have presided at the service. The meeting proceeded in a usual, though tense, manner, and the pastor preached from the text, "This is the victory which overcometh the world, even our faith."

The sermon was of a biblical nature and passed in Martin's usual storm-tossed style with no reference to the bishop's order.

The bishop appealed, so it was rumored, to Goering for help in ousting the pastor from his rectory, but this was refused because whatever else might have been said against the preacher, he was too good a patriot and too popular a war hero to be so lightly dismissed. The preacher stayed at his post, supported by a loyal congregation among whom were high officials of the Nazis.

The Confessional movement was gaining headway and all over Germany synods were being set up, whose basis was faith in Jesus Christ, as God's Son, and belief in the historic creeds or confessions of the Church. They refuted the heresies which the State religion encouraged among the people, such as the Nazis' claim to be the regulator of total human life. One of the six points laid down by the group was:

"The heresy is refuted that the state, over and above its special task, should and can become the single and total regulator of human life . . ."

Niemoeller assumed leadership of the movement's endeavors to block the bishop wherever possible, and wrote to him, saying, "We are now going to stand up against every action contrary to the Gospel by those who have forced the church to submit to their governmental violence—now, in a more decisive way than ever."

At a conventional meeting in Barmen, with two thousand representatives of six hundred Confessional groups or churches present, a declaration was formulated against the new German Christian order of religious activities. In this the voice of Niemoeller was never more decisive and challenging. Words could be no stronger than he used.

"The so-called national synod in Berlin"—the Nazi group headed by bishop Muller—"and its decisions

. . . are all invalid . . . Whosoever complies is . . . violating the laws of the church.

"The Reich church government despises the simple fundamentals of law and justice . . . It is devoid of that brotherly love made obligatory in the Holy Scriptures . . . forsakes the fundamentals of the Reformation church . . .

"Obedience to this church government is disobedience to God."

That was a history-altering moment, comparable to Luther's ringing challenge to the pope when he nailed his Ninety-five Theses on the Wartburg church door. Niemoeller had come out into the open and in doing so, defied death.

When the declaration was read, in approval the delegates stood and rang out Luther's Reformation song, "A Mighty Fortress Is Our God," which had become the battle charge of the Confessional Church. Niemoeller realized that he was fighting an enemy as bitter against true religion as Luther had fought when he challenged the pope. Well could he sing the words, as often he did in his own church:

> . . . The body they may kill,
> God's grace abideth still,
> His kingdom is forever.
> Let prince's or human favor depart
> If God's grace abide with me.
> Man's favor may come or not—
> But if not—let it to the Devil go!
> God's grace is enough for me.

Before the synodical meeting came to a close, a provisional church administration was set up with an executive council, in which Niemoeller became a

dominant light. On returning to his parish, he
realized that the first duty of himself, as well as of
the six thousand other pastors making up the Confessional Church leadership, must be to combat
through education and personal evangelism the German Christians and their pagan movement. Hence
his preaching took on something of the spiritual
fervor marking the Reformation Church.

His services rang with a spirit of evangelism and
a revival of personal piety. Whatever he did, whether
admonishing the congregation before his sermon began, leading them in his pastoral prayer, uniting in
the singing, reading the Scripture lesson, or delivering his messages, he swept the people before him into
a sense of God's nearness. Coming to grips with
Hitler had taught him how to touch the heavenly
spark which made his face and features glow with
the divine anointing.

Said a member of his congregation, "How can one
doubt that there is in him the spirit of Luther who
also fought against satanical powers and who wrote
the greatest fighting hymns the church ever possessed?" And this flaming spirit of his was to reach
the entire Confessional Church, so that a true revival
of religious interest took place among the pastors and
laymen. They realized with Martin they were fighting in God's battle to conserve religious freedom and
to combat a heresy unequalled in German history.

Herr Frick, minister of the Interior Department,
issued a decree in the fall of 1934 forbidding the pub-
lication of any news concerning the church struggle,
but this did not destroy the active work of the Confessional Church, which by October of that year was

fully organized as a national synod, with Martin's own parish going the full way.

Until March, of the following year, outward peace reigned as far as public knowledge of the inner mechanism of the Confessional Church was concerned. But the work of building a retaining wall against the new concept of German religion went steadily forward. Niemoeller never gave up the struggle for an instant, carrying it to his pulpit and into his parish through week-night meetings which crowded his building.

The battle flared forth in early March when the synod of the Prussian United Church, composed of the Lutheran and Reformed churches, a very conservative body, issued a manifesto or statement against Rosenberg's teachings of an eternal Germany. Rosenberg, cultural head of the Nazi party, had substituted an eternal Germany for the eternal Kingdom of God, in which only Aryans were members, and which was belabored with an eternal heritage of blessedness for faithful Aryan Nazis.

Niemoeller's spirit touched a spark to the smouldering fires of religious piety within this old conservative church, and they would have none of Rosenberg's German irreligion. They stated so, and against Krick's proclamation banning religious news from the press, they published their Manifesto. Krick flared forth with new bans and punishments for publishing it. He demanded that it should not be read from the pulpits.

And of course it was read publicly from those pulpits in hamlet and city. Faith and the martyr spirit were not dead in Germany, for there were many thousands of God-fearing, Hitler-hating pastors left.

On Sunday, March 10, Niemoeller before his morning sermon began to read this Protestant Manifesto to his congregation, as thousands of other ministers did. The people listened with profound attention as their spiritual leader stepped to the fore in this battle for God's Word and righteousness by faith in Jesus Christ—a concept finding no place among Rosenberg's new Germanic Christians.

"There is a bitter propaganda campaign against the church under way," the parson said to a crowded house. "We must fight against this, and for active, not passive, Christianity." He threw a depth charge into the religious sea of Nazism by his challenge, "The Jews are not the only ones who crucified Christ."

It was expected that Niemoeller on that Sunday would be molested, but he was not. His sermon went on as usual to a high climax, despite the fact that plain-clothes men from the Gestapo office entered the church and confiscated copies of the Manifesto.

The eyes of Christendom were upon Niemoeller that day. Dr. Samuel Trexler, in the Lutheran Church of the Transfiguration, New York City, said, "The protest of the churchmen of Germany planned for today calls for our attention and prayer. When he sank ships, he prayed for those who went down, for he was a Christian. But he would not bow to Ludwig Muller and fights with the same courage as when he was a submarine commander."

Niemoeller was not content with his charge against religious Hitlerism until he fired a salvo publicly at Rosenberg's *Mythology of the Twentieth Century,* a tirade against Christianity and a wild promulgation of German religion.

"In this new religion," said Niemoeller from his pulpit, "idols are made of blood and race. Faith in the eternal Germany demanded by this new religion is substituted for faith in the eternal kingdom of our Lord and Saviour, Jesus Christ. Such substitution makes God in the image of man and in it man honors, justifies and redeems himself. Such idolatry has nothing to do with positive Christianity. It is anti-Christ."

On that Sunday other pastors were not so favorably blessed as Niemoeller, their beloved leader, for the Gestapo arrested seven hundred for reading the Manifesto. The martyr in them stood forth and defied Hitler's black legions. Nor was Niemoeller lacking in such a spirit.

The storm really broke the following Sunday, March 17, when hundreds of churches were deprived of their ministers through arrest. Many of them were in prison. Five thousand preachers were affected. They were given the choice of arrest or signing an agreement not to read the protest against Hitler's idolatry or the new German Christians. Niemoeller did not schedule services for that day. When he arrived, the church doors were closed, and the crowd that had gathered stood with the pastor and sang their battle hymn, "A Mighty Fortress Is Our God." Their voices rang:

> A mighty fortress is our God,
> A bulwark never failing;
> Our helper He amid the floods
> Of mortal ills prevailing.

They were a people without a church—but not without a parson. Standing there, he joined his voice

2.8695

with theirs in this song which to them had become
a battle challenge.

The Gestapo arrested the pastor on the seventeenth,
but he was in no worse position than two hundred
other Berlin pastors who were arrested on the
previous Sunday for reading the Manifesto.

At St. Lucas in Berlin, after their regular preacher
had been arrested, on the second Sunday when the
German Christian preacher, supplied by the Hitler
group came in, the swastika was displayed. The
congregation rose and began singing, "A Mighty
Fortress Is Our God." When he stood forth to preach,
three-fourths of the audience left. This was the fate
of the Hitlerized German preachers, who were thus
forced to speak to empty pews for the most part.

Ralph Long, at the time executive secretary of the
National Lutheran Council, said, "The upheaval is
the result of the rationalistic tendency of higher
criticism."

The preacher's imprisonment, however, was of
short duration. For in his congregation was Count
Lutz Schwerin von Krosigk, a warm friend of the
Reich Finance Minister, who with other influential
members of the Dahlem parish prevailed with the
Nazi big-wigs to release Niemoeller. This was done
on the eighteenth.

During the summer Bishop Muller lost his grip on
the religious situation, and though aided by the
Gestapo was unable to hold the Confessional preachers in check. He tried to improve the Lord's Prayer
and to rewrite the Sermon on the Mount, which re-
sulted in a fierce revolt among the clergymen who
were faithful to the Word of God. Niemoeller's
actions threw this to the forefront, for he was con-

tinually on the watch for weak spots in the bishop's
armor.

Consequently the Reichsbishop was shorn of his
power on September 24, 1935. Martin thus had forced
Hitler's hand and caused a revocation of his trusted
church aide. The tilt was by no means over. For
the fuehrer determined to crush the Confessional
group at any price. He set up a Reich Ministry for
Church Affairs, headed by Hans Kerrl, with power
to set aside all church orders, constitutions and bring
them unconditionally under the Nazi yoke.

A month later Niemoeller, speaking before the
Pastors' Emergency League and the Prussian Synod,
referred to Hitler's last religious move, saying that
the directorate of the new Ministry was vested in
eight men. He bewailed the bringing of the swastika
dogmas into the Christian faith. To head this
National Church Committee Kerrl had called Bishop
Zoellner, the man who had given Niemoeller his first
important post in the church.

It was Zoellner's duty to bring about harmony
among the Nazi German Christians, the Confessional
Church and its leaders, and that large body of Luth-
erans who had remained neutral. Niemoeller at
heart wanted to work with him in this endeavor, but
he realized no compromise was possible with Nazism
as expressed by the new religious front. Consequently he lifted his voice in derision at this move
and publicly charged Hitler with bringing heresy
into the church.

The battle was on again—a battle in the end to be
won by Martin, though he was later to be arrested,
for he fought not with carnal but with spiritual
weapons. Each move Niemoeller made strengthened

the Confessional Synod, knit it into a closer unity, wove it into a fighting division, so that though the U-boat preacher was imprisoned, the group stands solidly against Hitler's encroachment upon true religious freedom in the Reich.

On the day Niemoeller addressed the Prussian Synod, it was rumored throughout Germany and splashed on the international news wires that Hitler called a Jewish doctor to treat an incipient cancer of the throat! Hitler might hate the Jew, but when his life depended upon Semitic skill, he quickly found a place in his thought (and irreligion) for the non-Aryan.

Chapter VII

CLASHING SWORDS WITH HITLER

RELIGIOUS conditions under Kerrl were much worse than when Muller as Reichsbishop was in charge of church affairs. The week following Niemoeller's address to the Pastors' Emergency League Kerrl told the ministers whom he had assembled for a conference that he would not tolerate their using the term heresy in church discussions. On Sunday, December 1, Niemoeller stood in his Dahlem pulpit and defied Kerrl's threat, and charged the government with introducing heresy into the Church of God.

His building was packed to the doors, for they were expecting their pastor to take up the cudgel against this new order. "It means that pure Christian doctrine alone," he said, "is to be suppressed and forbidden, for St. Paul in the Epistle to the Galatians wrote: 'If any man preach any other gospel unto you than that you have received let him be accursed.'"

He indicated that all Confessional pastors would make the same statement in their churches since other means of communication with the public had been closed to them. "The Brotherhood was informed last night by the Gestapo," he related, "that all announcements, reports, bulletins or communications to the Brotherhood Councils or to Synods or to the members of the same must be submitted to censorship."

This made it necessary for communications to be read directly to their congregations. Niemoeller looked upon the German Christian pastors as heretics trying to graft the Nazi doctrine into the Christian system. Hitler was saying that Christianity must be fought by the student shock troops "as an error that is destructive to society."

The following Thursday Hitler stepped into the battle and threatened to bring Niemoeller and his associates before the People's Tribunal, a criminal court, on charge of treason, and warned them that if they offered further opposition a treason trial would be faced at once by them.

This did not deter the fighting parson, but rather emboldened him. Nor was he afraid of Kerrl's latest move in depriving preachers of their salaries, as he had done with Bishop Otto Zenker of Silesia. He went a step farther and decreed that only State-controlled universities henceforth should be allowed to examine theological candidates. Sixty-two Rhineland preachers were cut off from their salaries, which stirred the Confessional preachers' ire.

On the following Sunday these pastors, headed by their former U-boat leader, planned a national disobedience day to Kerrl's orders. They sent out a general letter to be read on that Sabbath by the Confessional pastors in direct disregard of his command.

Niemoeller and all pastors reading the communication to their people thus faced death for treason, for they directly challenged Hitler's authority. On December 5 the Federal Council of Churches in America sent their official sympathy to Bishop August Marahrens of Hanover, a leading churchman of the nation.

December 6 Kerrl went a step farther and demanded that Niemoeller and the Confessional leaders give up their semi-official organization, which interfered with the administration of the Established Church. He required all pastors to come under the yoke of the State of which he was the church head, promising since Hitler did not want a State church that in two years he would withdraw and let the reunited Church run its affairs.

Niemoeller publicly countered that the Confessional pastors would not give up their battle until German Christians were removed from authority. Under Kerrl's charge the Gestapo seized the Confessional preachers' funds with which they were to carry on their fight.

As the Christmas season drew near Niemoeller expected some drastic action on Kerrl's part, nor was he to be disappointed. Gerhard Jacobi was scheduled to deliver his Christmas eve sermon in the Kaiser Wilhelm Memorial Church, one of Berlin's largest and most influential churches. The building was packed, the galleries filled and hundreds were turned away as this faithful leader in the opposition with Niemoeller was to speak.

Suddenly the Gestapo arrested the pastor, while German Christians took charge of affairs in the vestibule, where on a table were high piles of the Swastika Christian Journals, "Positive Christianity" and "The Gospel in the Third Reich" which were passed out to the people as they filed from the building after a substitute preacher had taken Jacobi's place.

Martin thoroughly expected a similar fate, though by a special dispensation from the Gestapo he was permitted to speak to the Dahlem congregation, but was expressly forbidden to preach outside of Berlin. Niemoeller's Christmas message was delivered with feeling and a sense of awe settling upon the hearers.

Hess became the official Nazi spokesman and said, in a Christmas eve broadcast, "A long time has passed since Germany could celebrate a peace as secure as the peace this year. A year ago I could not foresee that a kind fate would so soon make it possible for the fuehrer to proclaim Germany's liberty to return."

It was the rearming in defiance to the national powers of the world that was the seed from which World War II has sprung . . . a harsh fate inspired by the German god of war and not Niemoeller's Christian God.

During the week between Christmas and New Year the Confessional pastors were busy sending round robin or chain letters and bulletins in defiance of Kerrl's suppression and censorship of all church news. When Sunday, December 30, arrived Martin prepared his message with all diligence, working late into the early hours of the Sabbath that he might give expression to a spiritual hope for his people.

He was not, however, to deliver that message, for before service time the Gestapo arrived at his apartment and placed him under arrest to prevent his speaking. His arrest confined him to the apartment for the day. By this time he was no stranger to the secret police, for twice previously he had fallen into their clutches. The U-boat captain who had won the Iron Cross for bravery was not afraid to face Hitler's police.

Early in February, 1936, after two pastors had been arrested for slandering Rosenberg's advocacy of pagan Nordic myths, Martin came out of the vicarage of the Jesus Christus Kirche, walking with his sailor's rolling gait, and launched a one-man warfare against all forms of the German Christian dogmas. He was loud in damning as heresy their uniting of Christianity with Nazism.

"Loyal Protestants," he declared, "will make no compromise with Rosenberg." Nor was he willing to bow in obeisance to Kerrl, Hitler or the Gestapo, though it meant by not bowing to stand before the firing squad. His sermon of February 8 would have placed most Berlin pastors in prison, but by a special dispensation of God he was able to carry on the fight with immunity.

The year of 1936 was to be marked with diligence on Niemoeller's part in trying to check the Nazi encroachment upon true Christian faith. Before August arrived, many Confessional pastors and sympathizing preachers as well had been deprived of their churches; and German Christian pastors had been installed in their stead. Niemoeller saw this coming and recognized that Hitler's plan was to clear the churches of Christian preachers, loyal to the Bible and the historic creeds, and to substitute Nazi-fed pulpiteers.

The Confessional group worded a letter to be read by their pastors against this practice. On August 23 Niemoeller arose in his pulpit and read the letter as a stirring protest before a well-packed auditorium. Finished with the message, the congregation lifted the song, "A Mighty Fortress Is Our God." Martin was resting in this power, and though Hitler might seek his death, he was not afraid to stand forth in protest, as the author of the hymn had through protest given birth to Protestantism and the Lutheran Church.

"Only those fortunate enough to have been one of the congregation," wirelessed Guido Enderis to America, "and heard this moving presentation of the Confessional protest Manifesto . . . and then experienced the fervor with which the congregation sang Luther's battle hymn, can gauge the sincerity of that zeal or understand the emotion to which this quarrel has given rise."

Niemoeller was coming to explore something of the feelings with which Luther had produced Protestantism, and along with this famous sire of religious freedom, he too knew how to protest against the actions of those who sought to enslave the modern church.

On the anniversary of Luther's nailing his Ninety-five Theses to the church door, October 31, 1936, Niemoeller took for his text I Corinthians 2:2: "For I am determined not to know anything among you, save Jesus Christ, and him crucified." He described a picture which hung in the "revered village church at Dahlem." It was called "Luther Preaching," and was painted by a friend of Luther, Lucas Cranach.

In explaining the altar picture, Niemoeller told his congregation that the pulpit jutted out from the wall, and by it Luther was standing. On either side were men and women, kneeling or standing, listening to the preacher. In the middle stood a cross, and as the people listened to the speaker, their eyes were fixed on the cross, to which Luther was pointing.

"This is the work that God did through His servant Martin Luther," said Niemoeller, "in the German nation. He put the Cross with the Saviour back in the center again." Amid the gathering storm which at any moment might mean Martin's life, he was able to say, "We know, then, of the One who can help us. Be unto me a strong rock and defense that Thou mayest help me! For Thou art my rock and my fortress!"

Two weeks later in preaching on the Church, he said, "It may sound frightful and may well inspire us with horror to hear a high representative of the ruling power declare: 'National Socialism makes this claim in all seriousness: I am the Lord thy God. Thou shalt have no other gods beside me.' · This statement only makes it plain once more that it is impossible for Caesar's possessions . . . and God's to exist peacefully side by side, and that such an arrangement is not practicable for us."

On November 22, 1936, as the tragic events forced him to meet stolidly in the Christian faith any dangers which might be his lot, he said, "We are faced with the whole seriousness of death . . . To make terms with the enemy will not help us. Everything is at stake: it is the struggle of faith against unbelief, and there can be no yielding. We must go through with it. And we can lift up our heads because we have the one Lord who has borne the hate of the world, who has overcome the world and has not let Himself be overcome."

He faced 1937 with a determination to see his battle through at any cost. Not knowing how soon the Gestapo would arrest him, though sensing assuredly that it was on its way, he threw the whole power of his life into the fray. As Luther, he rejected all claims of the Nazi's spiritual dictatorship. He had built up such an influence that all of Germany listened to him, especially those of the Confessional groups.

When the Nazis purged the Jews and banned them from Christian church membership, Niemoeller cried out, "Those who have embraced our creed belong to us." When Hitler wanted to co-ordinate the churches and bring them under his dominance, he was the first to stand in opposition, declaring, "Render unto Caesar the things that are Caesar's, but unto God the things that are God's." When the Nazis began seizing church money he said, "The seizure of power began with the confiscation of church finances." And as Hitler's clutches settled over the German churches, Niemoeller arose to challenge, "Hands off the Evangelical Church of the German Reich."

Things were drawing to a quick conclusion. For years he knew his life was in danger, but when denied the privilege of preaching, he preached anyway. When other pastors were arrested, he carried on the battle with added vigor. The more the church was oppressed, the higher he lifted his voice in reprisal. The State ministry denied the Confessional churches the privilege of receiving collections, but Martin Niemoeller took collections—the largest ever gathered in the Reich. Kerrl said, "You must not organize classes for theological students." But he organized and conducted them himself.

One of the problems of the Confessional Church was the training of their ministry. Seminaries had been taken over by the State, and candidates for the ministry were examined only by Nazi-controlled professors, which created a tragedy for Niemoeller and his associates. However, he was not to be deterred by such a ban, and he organized his own seminary classes, as other pastors did; and all of them secretly supported banned seminaries and their teachers.

To meet the increased pressure from Hitler, Niemoeller conducted week-night parish meetings where hundreds flocked to hear him. He knew every word spoken was reported by Nazi spies and secret agents. But he told the gestapo officers that he despised them and hoped they would hear something of the true gospel while in his meetings.

Many people were perplexed by the difficulties they faced, the issues at stake; and on coming to their pastor, he invited all who would discuss these problems with him to a meeting at the parsonage. At first a small group sat around his table, but soon the crowd outgrew the parsonage and moved into the parish house hall where six to eight hundred people gathered nightly.

Other Confessional pastors followed the same plan. Niemoeller laid down strict regulatory rules for those who might attend these meetings. Only those were permitted to enter who had a membership card in the Confessional Church, issued on condition of belief in the creed, a faithful adherence to Reformation doctrines and a willingness to sacrifice for this belief.

Pastors gave these cards out, but often the secret police were able to obtain them. The Gestapo prided themselves in 1937 that they held more than forty parish-hall entrance tickets.

Pastor Niemoeller at first invited the people to hear the latest religious news and to lay before them plans for the Confessional Church struggle, but later he added Bible study to the meetings. He wished to instruct his people in a knowledge of the confessions, the creed and the Bible. These groups came to be called "Confirmation Classes for Adults," when for an hour they studied the Bible together.

The struggle was slowly telling on Martin's physical man. He lost his youthful appearance, his glowing optimistic outlook, and was bent under the load of the church which he oversaw.

He espoused the cause of a church free from political domination, and could not rightly be accused of treason because he brought gospel messages to reassure his people and to strengthen their faith for all eventualities. The reason he was able to continue his preaching during the first half of 1937 was because of his influential members' power in the Reich.

However turbulent the days, tiresome the weeks, or storm-tossed the months, Niemoeller always made exacting sermonic preparation. He stood as one between the living and the dead and he dared not enter the pulpit with less than God's best message for his people. He selected his text for each Sunday from the designated scripture according to the Lutheran ritual. Due to emergencies and Nazi orders he would be required to work until one or two o'clock on Sunday mornings that his sermon might receive its finishing touches under the glow of a trouble-seared life whose faith was in God.

As a conscientious shepherd of his flock, no persecution from the Gestapo nor orders from the State could force him to give up holding his own confirmation classes. As often as four mornings a week he met the future members of the church at eight o'clock in the parish house. Twice weekly he held confirmation classes from three to seven in the afternoon.

When the Hitler Youth organization became all-encompassing, he lengthened his confirmation classes from one to two years of study, that he might offset the Nazi influences over his young people. Other pastors followed this practice.

Nor was he ever too busy to break his rule of reserving midafternoons for funerals, weddings and other parish calls, hundreds of which came to him from Berlin's four million people. Noontime often found the Dahlem pastor at some conference or council meeting of the Confessional Church leaders. When free from engagements in his own parish on week-nights he was speaking in distant cities, returning by sleeper that he might be in time to meet his eight o'clock confirmation class.

When Hitler's "stooges" suspended a pastor, Niemoeller was the first to render aid, raising money for their dependents and consoling them in whatever way possible. Gifts for this purpose were so plentiful that he declared "money lies on the streets."

Niemoeller the man was thoroughly human, finding his chief delight in his family of seven children. He looked to Frau Else for constant comradeship, and when he had finished writing in longhand his Sunday sermons he read them to her in the quiet of the parsonage for criticism, thinking doubtless that it was better for her to exercise her critical prerogative before delivery than after. He discussed his texts with her and the selection of the hymns for each service. After his early morning meal on Sundays he returned to his desk where he stayed until service time.

In the midst of his busy career, challenging Hitler's religious paganism, meeting the problems of building a Confessional Church organization to withstand the time when he should be imprisoned, Martin was possessed of a driving urge. "Pastor Niemoeller lives and fights for one thing, to preach the Gospel as long as he has time and a place and strength of body and soul for the duty," writes a Swiss comrade-in-arms.

He has always been marked with the characteristic of knowing what he wanted and where he was going. This Westphalian "thickskulledness," determination to carry on to the end, was the secret of his human strength to endure in this fight against Nazi encroachment upon the church.

His pastoral work was of a serious nature, and even when the demands of the Confessional groups became time-consuming he still could be seen racing through Berlin's streets, driving his automobile on some Christian errand. He never used a chauffeur, driving himself, usually with one hand, carefully, yet with grimness in his face. A friend says that he wore out a car in two years, and bought a new one just before his imprisonment, prepared to keep up the terrific pace of his work.

Toward the end he crystallized his contention with the Hitlerized church program in five points. He felt first that the church alone was able to judge what pastors were to be removed or retained, that it had a time-honored right to train its own youth, and that the Word of God was not bound as Hitler-paganism declared it to be. Secondly, he defied Nazism on the basis of man's nature, declaring him to be in need of redemption, which act must be accomplished for him through Christ. He believed as Barth, the Swiss theologian, declares, "Life is not achieved by deeds, but rather by forgiveness of sins."

Thirdly, he was in direct opposition to the Nazi's defiance and mockery of the Christian sacraments, which Martin held to be instituted by the early Church and biblically founded. Fourthly, he looked upon the Bible as God's Word, which of course the Nazis denied; and finally, the Nazi ethics that might makes right he found to be in contradiction to the Bible.

This was a battle to death in which he had engaged. Martin had never learned the meaning of surrender. The spirit that caused him to refuse to tow submarines to Scapa Flow now propelled him indomitably to see the end of this fight for conscience and right. He was not alone in this battle, being sustained by the brotherhood of hundreds of Confessional preachers, the prayers of his flock and the hand of God.

He opened 1937 by saying in his New Year sermon on January 1, "But the one eternal God has stretched out His hand to us and that hand will not let us go; the eternal God has given His word—and that word does not deceive ... If we believe Him, dear brethren, if we know that we are safe in His hands, how can we possibly act as though He were not the Lord to whom all power belongs in Heaven and on earth?"

In the midst of his distress, he was upheld by an unfaltering faith in the final rightness of things and found his labors glorious. He said, "Yes, in beginning a new year we are called to a happy work, dear brethren. We know not what it may bring; but one thing we do know: the eternal God is faithful and gracious and He will not let the work of His hands go."

Around the bend of the year were heartaches unknown before, persecution and imprisonment; but skylighting it was the all-pervading sense of being in the right relationship to God's will. He walked with his head toward the heavens, though at any moment he expected death.

CHAPTER VIII

MARCHING TOWARD PRISON

NIEMOELLER, though he knew his arrest was but a matter of moments, did not give up the fight as he entered into the new year. Nor did he alter the tenor of his sermons, which until his last remained simple Gospel messages for the encouragement of his people, as well as for the spiritual enlightenment of those who were not of the Christian fold.

In late January the German Christians seized control of the churches in Lubeck, in defiance of Dr. Zoellner. Nine Confessional pastors were arrested and when Dr. Zoellner, head of the National Church Committee, set up by Kerrl, sent one of his trusted associates to the city, he also was arrested. Determining to go himself and discharge the usurping Kerrl preachers, he was turned back by the Gestapo. This caused him to resign, and showed that Niemoeller was right when he refused to be associated with his old superintendent on the Kerrl committee. The grand old man, disheartened and disillusioned, died shortly afterward.

Preaching on the last Sunday in January, 1937, Niemoeller referred to the incident. He said, "We are gathered as a Christian congregation to hear the Word of God"—the heart of the pastor's messages. "What really depresses us is the irrefutable fact that during these years the Church itself has been made prisoner, that the Church itself has lost its freedom to carry out its mission. It would be lying, were we to attempt to assert that the Evangelical Church is today freely permitted to preach the message which it is ordered to preach.

"The one word 'Lubeck' speaks too plainly for its import to be missed: Lubeck, the town in Germany where the preaching of the biblical Gospel is forbidden by police; Lubeck, the town in the Fatherland where all evangelical preachers have been forcibly prevented by the police from bearing witness to the Lord Jesus Christ as the one Saviour and Redeemer . . . Where is all this leading? . . .

"A captive Church, a Church without liberty, and the Church is still on trial. No man can say when and how this trial will end . . . in acquittal or in the death sentence."

On February 28, in both St. Anne's and the Church of Jesus Christ, Niemoeller announced that Weissler, secretary of the National Confessional Synod, who had been arrested sometime previously, had died in the Sachsenhausen concentration camp, where he was found hanging in his cell. The inference was that he had committed suicide.

"A few of us had the tragic duty," he told his congregations, "some days ago of standing by his coffin and we have been told that our brother-in-the-faith had taken his own life. But we who know him, know this could not be true." There was a visible stir in the pews—as also a thunderous rumble throughout the Confessional Church—and the pastor proceeded with his prayers, after which he read the list of thirteen imprisoned or exiled pastors for whom he asked the congregation to lift their petitions Heavenward.

Outlining something of Hitler's plan for a new church election, which he called a "free election," Niemoeller said, "Protestantism will soon abandon connection with the State. There can be no religious freedom, and no freedom of the press during the coming church elections. You must accustom yourselves to make voluntary offerings to the church. This is a struggle between Satan and Jesus of Nazareth."

Speaking from the passage, "He that is not with me is against me, and he that gathereth not with me scattereth abroad," he declared, "Hitler is attempting to create a church, his German Christian church, made up of 'moderate Christians' on the one hand and moderate heathen on the other."

Well-meaning neutrals came in for their denunciation, as he affirmed such churchmen would be numbered among this heathen class unless they heeded Jesus' invitation, "Come unto me."

Martin was fighting intensely, determinately, for the cause which he believed to be one of life and death. In an effort to present his views to the public more clearly, he wrote a pamphlet, "We Summon Germany to God," which when it appeared was confiscated by the Gestapo. The previous Sunday evening preaching on "The Church of Christ," he said, "Christian men and women are offering up their lives for Jesus Christ—even in the literal sense . . . No friendship or brotherliness, no Christian solidarity, negotiating with the world in order to reconcile it, or wrestling with it in order to overcome it, is here of any use."

His encounter with the Gestapo because of his pamphlet was a nerve-racking experience, and so he

was absent from his pulpit for the following two
Sundays; but when he spoke again on Sunday the
twenty-fourth, he confessed he had been tormented
and oppressed by the thought that all this wordy
striving against the enemy of the Church was useless. "Who today," he asked, "still dares to hope for
a happy ending to the cause of Jesus Christ in our
nation? Who can muster up the confidence to believe in such an ending?"

Referring to the chained Bibles in Luther's day, he
avowed, "We have all that directly before our eyes;
we can see how God's Word is being put into chains
and imprisoned from the list of undesirable books on
which figures nearly all the desirable Christian
literature, to the prison-cells which close behind the
messengers of Jesus Christ, even to the prayers . . .
that God may give our people back the free and un-
impeded preaching of the gospel."

Again he made mention of the coming church elections, which he was certain would be as Hitler's
previous election when Muller was "railroaded" into
the bishop's office. He made it clear that however
the elections came out, the Confessional group had
no intention of remaining in the same church with
the German Christians.

Niemoeller knew that every time he made these
public statements from his pulpit, he was hastening
the hour when the Gestapo would arrest him. And
there was no reason for him to look for a fate any
better than that of Weissler, the supposed suicide,
who in reality had been Gestapo-murdered. But this
made no alteration in the plain course of his work.
He had set his face flintily toward declaring the un-
trammeled Gospel as he saw it, come fair or foul

weather, come Gestapo, a concentration camp, and death.

When Kerrl threw before the churchmen his new expression of Hitler's religious authority, Niemoeller could not restrain his religious indignation. Kerrl said, "The National Socialist Party represents a positive Christianity. The question of the divinity of Christ is ridiculous and unessential. A new authority has arisen as to what Christ and Christianity really are—Adolf Hitler."

Shortly a fresh tirade came from Kerrl's office in the form of a ban on public collections for special work among the Confessional churches. Following this, Niemoeller and his fellow churchmen refused publicly to recognize Kerrl's right to have any authority over the Church.

They mailed a new proclamation of their stand to Confessional pastors throughout the nation, saying, "Either we are to have an evangelical church based on God's Word and faith in Christ or we are to have a religious association (the new German national church) based on a new revelation which has confused the duties of church and state and which must entirely forfeit every claim to call itself the Protestant church . . .

"Either we are followers of Christ, or we are to take the road which surrenders bit by bit the truth revealed in the Bible and ends in a substitute faith in Germany. We must face this question frankly and let no effort to cloud the issue deceive us."

This was playing with fire. Niemoeller had defied Reichsbishop Muller to such an extent that Hitler had to take matters out of his hands and place them in a new appointee, whom he personally selected to keep the Confessional group controlled. And now this parson who was not afraid of death was defying Kerrl, and had backed him so far from the center of religious authority that Hitler himself was calling for another "free religious election." The battle resolved into a duel between Niemoeller and Hitler . . . the first, the highest authority in the Confessional, fighting-for-the-faith Church, and the other, the highest dictatorial power in the State.

There could be but one end, and that was death for Martin. Either this or Hitler would lose his first internal, national battle; and once his authority had been challenged, and the contending party had gotten away with it, no one could tell from what source the next challenger would step forth.

The parson set himself against those free elections with all the dynamite of his soul and all the experience of his previous years of battling against religious usurpation of authority by the State.

In Martin's May 2 Sunday sermon, he aroused his people to the tragedy of meeting the religious situation complacently, saying, "I tell you, the danger is great," and went on to outline the problems which faced the youth of that hour.

His Whitsunday sermon was banned because of his flagrant opposition to the religious policy of the Reich, though he did deliver a Whitmonday sermon in which he spoke about the battle cry of the German Christians being, "A National Church." They were calling, he informed his Monday evening congregation, for "a de-confessionalization of the church."

"Behind such slogans as 'De-confessionalization! National Church!' there lies concealed the intention to do away altogether with the Christian Church and

the Christian faith," rang out his voice in the parish
house.

June was ushered in by Niemoeller's making a
series of speeches against the coming elections. On
the fourth he publicly warned his people to be on
their guard against them. The printed notices of
his meetings were seized by the police, as were also
all published records and excerpts from his talks.

"The position of the church today is precarious,"
he said. "Inside it is empty and only the walls remain. The question now is whether these last remaining walls will be torn down . . . or whether they
will be dismantled stone by stone." He denounced
as diabolical the popular conception which the German Christian leaders were fostering that "the
nation must be freed of Jesus Christ." Nor could he
close the address without a reference to the thirty
Protestant leaders who had recently been arrested,
upon whom he looked as true Christian martyrs,
willing to give their lives rather than deny their
Lord.

On June 9 a report was wirelessed from London to
America concerning von Ribbentrop's attempt to join
Niemoeller's church. While in Germany he had
severed his relationship with the Church altogether,
as had many of Hitler's trusted allies. But on arriving in London, where he went as an ambassador, his
friends informed him that he would have better suc-
cess by connecting himself with a large church group,
as a great many of the leading English officials were
churchmen.

Residing in the Dahlem parish, with which he had
formerly been connected, his application for membership was referred to Niemoeller by the Berlin

Bishop's Consistory. The fighting parson was reported to have said in answering:

"Excellency: Your application to return to the Church has been duly received. Before dealing with its contents, I beg you to inform me whether the step is prompted by religious conviction or is due to political consideration?"

"Reasons of state," came the ambassador's answer.

Back went Niemoeller's, "Insufficient reasons for joining the church." And the case was dismissed from the parson's mind. That was his caliber. Martin was beholden to Jesus Christ and only through faith in Christ could one become a member of his new Confessional Church, State reasons notwithstanding. Looking upon God as his Fuehrer, he was not afraid to say, even to Hitler himself, that by faith in Christ alone are the church doors open for entrance.

Only the man who dared preach as Niemoeller preached on the Sunday previous to his clash with von Ribbentrop could withstand the pressure of Hitler's aides and his secret police. He said in his sermon on "Seek Ye the Lord":

"No man must be ashamed—not even a German needs be ashamed—when God calls us to repentance; but we should be ashamed—every German and every other man—when, lest we be laughed at, we take up a vainglorious attitude and listen to human voices because of our fear of men, and are ashamed to repent, but fall with open eyes into the pit from which God's call is trying to save us."

He concluded his message, "We should take the signs of the times to mean that the decisions demanded of us by God cannot be postponed, for there

is a 'Too late!' . . . which leaves us nothing to hope
for, when the sands of the last 'today' have run out."

On June 17 it was announced that half of the
governing council of the Prussian Confessional
Church had been arrested and the others were in
hiding lest they suffer a similar fate. On that night
Niemoeller was speaking in the parish house, for it
was Friday. The crowds came early, packed the
hall, and hundreds were turned away. Instead of
leaving, they insisted that the pastor deliver his message a second time. After finishing his first message,
the hall emptied and was filled with the waiting
people, and he spoke to them on the same subject.

At the close of the second service a group of the
Hitler Youth stepped up and said, "Cease collecting
money for this club. It is forbidden." They referred, of course, to the collection which the pastor
was taking to carry on the work of the Confessional
Synod. While the uproar was going on, the Christians lifted their battle hymn, "A Mighty Fortress Is
Our God," which they continued singing until the
police arrived and forced the Hitler Youth away.

"The present Protestant Church situation is hope-
less from the worldly standpoint. No one knows who
will be arrested next," he said. Referring to the
church elections, he continued, "I cannot imagine
what sort of election it is going to be. The situation
has become more threatening than ever during the
past few days. The Confessional Church will not of
course take part in such church elections. Today
the administration of the church is in the hands of
a political ministry.

"The Reich Church Minister regards faith in Jesus
Christ as an absurd side issue, and his right hand

man, his State Secretary, announced his resignation from the church just a week before he was called to the post. These are the men who now govern the Protestant Church of Germany.

"Threatened before everything else is our Protestant youth work. The newspapers have announced that in the new Hitler schools no religious instruction is given. Missions director Lockis of Berlin has been arrested. Three theological students have been expelled from the University of Berlin because they attended courses given by the Confessional Synod. Forty-three out of the forty-six professors of theology on our university faculties are German Christians, teaching that Christ was an Aryan.

"We have reached the end. We do not need to worry any more about Church reform. These matters have been taken out of our hands. We were to have had free elections. Now the free elections have become exactly the contrary. Only church enemies are free.

"But I assure you that the church is not at an end . . . We will not surrender our rights."

The following Sunday he preached on "The Salt of the Earth," delivering a warm-hearted, tender and soul-searching message. He prefaced his introduction by a five-minute reading of the list of arrested people, which he called his "Intercessory List," and of which he had been forbidden to speak.

He referred to what he called the "shockingly long list" of seventy-two or seventy-three names of persons, known and unknown, pastors and church members, who had been arrested. "No one can say whether the list is complete and each of us has a foreboding that it will become larger still, as it has grown in the week past. What are these pastors and church members accused of?" He outlined something of their faith, which was the basis of their arrest, saying: "God be praised and thanked: our brothers and sisters cannot be reproached with the slightest trace of anything conventionally reprehensible; but on the contrary these people have been banished from their homes, condemned to be silent and thrown into prison, because they considered it their duty and because they claimed it the right of the Evangelical Church to denounce attacks against the Christian faith freely . . . and to denounce interference with Christian worship fearlessly as interference."

He openly challenged Hitler in this sermon with his early promise that the church would not be shackled. He asked, "Does the fuehrer's word still hold good?" Outlining the situation in Berlin and elsewhere as to the causes of pastors being arrested, he said on reading his text, "Ye are the salt of the earth; ye are the light of the world":

"When I read these words today, they became really new to me, and I had to go back and reread them; and I had a feeling of inward relief . . . The *Gospel* must remain the *Gospel;* the *Church* must remain the *Church;* the *Creed* must remain the *Creed* . . . And we must not—for Heaven's sake—make a German Gospel out of the Gospel; we must not make a German Church out of Christ's Church; we must not make *German* Christians out of the Evangelical Christians."

He said that he was accosted on all sides by statesmen as well as by "the man in the street" who told him, "For God's sake, do not speak so loudly or you

will land in prison. Pray do not speak so plainly:
surely you can also say all that in a more obscure
fashion."

Niemoeller retorted, "We are not allowed to put
our light under a bushel; if we do we are disobedient
. . . It is no business of ours whether the Church continues to live and is not put to death . . . I must speak
today; for perhaps I shall no longer be able to do so
next Sunday . . . who knows what next Sunday may
bring forth? . . .

"And so when it comes to the election, we shall not
mix up the salt, we shall not put the light in the
corner, but shall say, as God's Word says, 'Heaven
and earth shall pass away—but the Word of God
does not pass away' . . . Happy is he who accepts
this grace . . . so that he stands firmly established
though the storms may roar and the waters rise."

As though he recognized the gathering storm about
to break upon him, he delivered his message in
language as warm as it could be brewed in his own
heart, and in words as soul-strengthening as he
knew. He might have suspected it, though he was
not certain, that he had but one more sermon to
deliver before his arrest.

On the next Monday Goebels made a fiery and
denunciatory speech against religion, declaring, ". . .
we have too many churches." He ridiculed church
leaders, and accused the Catholics of being sexual-
ists, a common political charge made by the Nazis
that they might arrest priests and nuns in disregard
of all other charges or offences.

Niemoeller announced on the same day there had
been many more arrests of the faithful and said that
at three o'clock that morning the Gestapo had sur-

rounded the home of Pastor Asmussen, but since he had fled, they arrested his wife. "I alone am free as yet," he stated. In speaking of the church elections which had been officially announced for the following Sunday, he was firm in his avowal that the Confessional Church members would ignore them.

Hitler faced a fiery and dynamite-packed problem in those elections. If he held them and the Confessional Church did not vote, then he had lost his victory, even though his nominees, or shall I say *appointees* were elected as certainly they would be. And if he canceled the elections or postponed them, as he did, and Niemoeller remained free, his authority in church matters had been crushed upon the rock that was Niemoeller.

It was either Niemoeller's arrest or cancel the elections. And this Hitler as a master strategist knew.

One evening during the week while Martin was in conference with a visitor at the parsonage, his ten-year-old son ran into the room and said, "I have had such a dreadful dream about you, father." Without permitting the preacher to inquire about it, the lad broke out, "I dreamed the Gestapo came to take you away."

"But, son," said the preacher, "God will take care of me."

"Oh, father, can God take care of you in a concentration camp?" Being assured that He could, the lad left the room satisfied that though his father should be arrested, he was in God's hands.

When Martin's last free Sunday arrived, he was ready for his pulpit, with a sermon which had taken shape in the wee hours of Sunday morning. He planned to speak on Gamaliel's advice: ". . . if it be

of God, ye cannot overthrow it." Reading the list of
the imprisoned for whom prayer was offered as the
congregation stood, he launched into his sermon,
mingling the current situation with the similar one
which arose in Jesus' time.

In the Friday paper, he informed the people, there
was an article against the Confessional Church under
the heading of "Incitement to Insubordination." "At
the end of the newspaper article, which is written to
make trouble, it says: 'Another clergyman escaped
arrest by taking flight.' This remark can apply to no
one else but our brother pastor Asmussen. A week
ago he left Berlin on my advice and on the implicit
instruction of his superiors."

Then he went on to relate how he had written the
Reich Minister of Justice informing him that
Asmussen would be at his service as soon as a writ
of subpoena was served or a warrant issued for his
arrest. The Minister of Justice answered, "We have
sent a copy of your letter to the Gestapo."

Niemoeller boldly threw the facts before the public
undaunted by fear of the outcome, saying, "We have
as little thought and hope as the Apostles had of
escaping from the clutches of the powers-that-be by
our own efforts; and we have certainly as little intention as they had of obeying the human command
to keep silent regarding what the Lord our God
orders us to say; for as long as the world shall last,
one must obey God rather than man."

He boldly told his people of the persecutions which
during the past three weeks had become as machine-
gun fire. The Gestapo had broken into churches,
ousted pastors, arrested women members of the Saar-
brucken congregation, "because they were distribut-

ing an election leaflet of the Confessional Church at the request of the Council of Brethren." Churches were empty of people and pastors because the ruthless Gestapo had taken them into custody without the formality of charges or trial.

He referred to the Communion Service, held on Friday evening, when sitting beside him were three young members of the Gestapo, "who came in their official capacity to spy . . . who were assuredly baptized once in the name of the Lord Jesus Christ and vowed loyalty to their Saviour at the confirmation altar."

His building was crowded at both services and he again spoke of the fact that he alone of the Confessional Synod was free, avowing, "I will continue to fight for the Confessional Church though I am the only leader left. This is a struggle of the State against the Church."

It was understood by those who were close to the Nazis that the Gestapo had orders that Niemoeller was not to be molested, whatever he said or did, without Hitler's personal authorization.

"As for us we think no more of evading the orders of the authorities than did the Apostles. We think no more thereof than we do of denying that which our God and our Saviour ordered us to do." His sermon rang with the challenge of God's Word which had always prevailed, and which he took as his personal marching orders.

"It may be a good thing that this is no pleasure excursion," he climaxed his last message, "and that the way of the Cross cannot be learned overnight. It may be just as well that the road is long and difficult, otherwise we might confuse our pious moods,

our loyalty to our convictions, our manly courage . . .
with faith, which is a gracious gift from God and
which He bestows upon us through the Holy Ghost.

"But on this long and difficult road we may learn,
in the bitterness of tribulation, to pay attention to
the Word of our Lord, and so we may begin in earnest
to hear and preach and teach the Word of the Cross,
the Gospel of Jesus Christ, without ceasing.

"Our duty—and we have no other—is that we
should be like the Apostles, who when a new embargo
was laid upon their preaching, went forth and did
not cease to preach . . . the message of the Cross . . .
For it is by this Word—and by this Word alone—
that our faith lives . . .

"Dear friend, man does not live by bread alone,
but by the Word of God."

At the close of the evening service, he took a collection for the Confessional work, dismissed his congregation and returned to the parsonage.

He had preached his last sermon with the fervency
of a soul white-hot and flaming with Divine truth.
He feared not the face of man, receiving his orders
only from the Commander of his faith.

Goebels, doubtless hearing of Niemoeller's sermon,
remarked in a speech he made that day, "Why don't
preachers preach and be obedient to the State?"

He had marched through his last free Sunday
straight toward prison, and knew it, unmoved by
fear. Hitler might imprison his body, but he could
not shackle his soul.

That final sermon was broadly published, and dis-
tributed outside of Germany. One copy from which
many translations have been made appeared in the
"Neues Tage-Buch," the Paris-German emigre week-

ly. Boiling out of the tragedy of his life, it matches in import the sermons of Luther. His last twenty-eight sermons have been published under the title of *God Is My Fuehrer,* and may well stand beside those of the famous Reformation sire.

They ring with a trueness to the Word of God, upon which they are based, for in the final analysis the Confessional Church had this one distinctive difference from the German Christian group: the first was a Bible-founded church, while the latter cast aside God's Word, substituting for it the cunningly devised fables of Germany's Rosenbergs, Mullers, Kerrls—its Hitlers, Goerings, Goebels. Amid the din which these pagan-minded men made, Martin lifted his voice to proclaim the Word of the Lord, as living, enduring, eternal in its demands upon men's souls. To Niemoeller the Bible was his marching orders.

CHAPTER IX

IN THE HANDS OF THE GESTAPO

HITLER weighed carefully every chance. Years before he told Niemoeller that for him it was either the dictator's orders or the firing squad. But the longer the fuehrer waited, the stronger Niemoeller became, until for three years he dared not arrest and imprison his No. 1 religious enemy. Knowing the suddenness with which the Gestapo acted on the slightest provocation, the fuehrer made certain they would make no unwise movement with reference to the popular parson of the influential Dahlem parish by giving them strict orders not to molest the preacher without a command from himself.

He knew in the end that Niemoeller's influence and grip on the souls of faithful Germans must be broken. He had hoped for a free church election which would cause the parson's popularity to wane. But when the appointed date set for the elections approached, Hitler's nerve failed him, and he cancelled them. To the final day of arrest he sought a way to break Martin's spirit without police action and court sentence.

But he found none, for in the soul of this man of God ran the blood of martyrs, who would gladly die for Christ's cause. Hitler would have slain him had he possessed enough nerve to face the uprising among Niemoeller's countless thousands of followers. Next to the firing squad, as a solution, was the concentration camp. And on July 1 Hitler gave the arrest order.

Early in the morning several Gestapo agents found him at home with his family. Two of the police detained him, while the others searched his wife and children in another room. Martin could hear the excited voices of his family and the weeping of the younger children during the several hours when the searching was going on. Finally he was taken to the Gestapo headquarters, where he was rushed into the presence of an official.

On expressing indignation at the manner of his arrest and treatment he was informed that it was all his fault. "We have taken notice of your attitude toward the fuehrer," said the officer, to be countered by Niemoeller's, "I have defended the Church against the attack, which is my duty."

Hitler's desire was to gain a compromise from the fiery preacher, whose denunciations he feared as much as an enemy army; and to do this he hoped to have Martin sign a statement that as his future policy he would no longer fight the Nazi church's dictatorial regime but would co-operate with the State's decisions in religious matters.

Niemoeller's emphatic *"No!"* rang through the room. He who had refused to tow submarines to England dared not break faith with the Confessional martyrs and those who had not yet felt Hitler's keen-edged ax upon their necks.

When the love of the Fatherland was thrown in his teeth, he was quick to point out the fact that he had undertaken many dangerous trips in a U-boat to save his country, and could not be accused of an indifference to her present fate.

Having been arrested on a bench warrant, he was taken before the issuing judge of the criminal court, or the People's Tribunal, for preliminary hearing, which proved to be more of a farce or "frame-up" than a hearing.

Nor had the Gestapo left his office without having fleeced it of 12,000 marks which had been taken up as church offerings to carry on the Confessional synodical battle. He learned that his Dahlem church office had also been sealed and the pastor's personal documents confiscated.

Though under arrest Niemoeller had the consciousness of having done all in his power for the Confessional Church in preparing her to carry on though the executive officers had been arrested. Knowing that a concentration camp awaited him and his brethren in the Confessional leadership, he had effected a secretive administrative organization which could function though all the previous leaders and officers were imprisoned or murdered.

On his last free Sunday he told his congregation that such a catacomb body of overseers had been created to carry on their fight against Hitler's religious policy. He could look back upon that Sunday without any searing of conscience, for he had done his best. Monday night before his arrest he had boldly faced the coming issues, and taken his congregation to his heart of affection. They had stood by him through the death struggle and in the end he was not willing to deflect one iota from his original course of fighting this pagan monster which was fast sucking the blood from the Christian Church, and turning her into a defeated Aryan society of heathen.

He said that the present intolerable church struggle

had been brought on because of the one issue: Could Hitler's word be trusted?

Among his very close sympathizers at the moment were Finance Minister Von Krosigk, a member of his church with Confessional leanings, and Dr. Hjalmar Schact, president of the Reichsbank, through whose influence Niemoeller's arrest had doubtlessly been postponed numerous times.

The State on making the arrest issued the following notice to the press:

"Pastor Niemoeller has over a long period made agitatory addresses in both divine services and public assemblies; has slandered leading figures in the state and the party and has spread untrue assertions regarding measures taken by the State with the purpose of disturbing the citizens. He has likewise urged opposition to the State's laws and ordinances.

"His assertions were a constant feature of the anti-German foreign press."

This last charge later was flatly denied by Niemoeller, who affirmed that at no time had he given interviews with foreign newspaper men—though, of course, the Martin-against-Adolf duel had been lionized by the press the world over. The German papers, not then so completely subsidized by the Nazi regime as at present, did its share in giving Niemoeller's arrest proper front-page recognition.

The day after the arrest his wife was permitted to visit him in the prison where he was temporarily lodged. It was a touching meeting of these two faithful lovers; yet in the end Frau Else returned to the parsonage to carry on to the best of her ability the work of home and parish, awaiting Martin's release—for which she prayed but which did not loom as a possibility upon her mental horizon.

On the same day the public press was loudly berated by the Gestapo for emphasizing the sordid facts of the arrest—facts which they wanted to forget and erase from public memory as soon as possible.   A Nazi official let it be known that if there were additional unwelcomed Niemoeller or Confessional Church publicity, the press would also be called before the criminal court for more than a mental "dusting-off."

In spite of Hitler's clamping tight the lid upon all Niemoeller publicity newspaper, boatloads of it have slipped under the ban. A few prisoners who have been with him in jail and in concentration camps, later to be released, have brought with them an inkling of Niemoeller's treatment. Some of this is well-authenticated; some is of doubtful origin and truth; and to say the least some is not to be accepted at full face value by a gullible, sensation-loving public. However, there are reliable sources of information which truthfully give us a picture of Martin's life, at least in parts; and above all, his twice-monthly letters to his wife and her infrequent visits vividly picture his concentration-camp life.

On the first Sunday of his incarceration, he sent words of cheer to his congregation from the Moabit prison. At the church Professor Dibelius, the day's preacher, spoke to two morning congregations—so great were the crowds. He read the absent pastor's message, admonishing the Confessional Church not to be downhearted but to sing hymns of courage and joy.

This was climaxed by a message to the people from the Secret Confessional Synod, denying flatly the State's charges against Niemoeller. At the close of the services hundreds of signatures were placed on a petition to the Minister of Justice, requesting their pastor's release. Before presenting the petition, Professor Bachnin, chairman of the parish council, warned the people that it might fall into the hands of the Gestapo, in spite of which three-fourths of the congregation signed.

Women wept unconstrainedly during the church services. Professor Dibelius said, "The beloved, courageous and upright pastor of this church is in prison. We here in this house will pray for his welfare and the day of his return. The parishioners can do little for him now, except pray that God will give him a firm heart." He concluded his sermon by quoting from Paul's famous words:

"Who shall separate us from the love of Christ? Shall tribulation, or distress, or persecution, or famine, or nakedness, or peril, or sword?

"As it is written, For thy sake we are killed all the day long; we are accounted as sheep for the slaughter . . .

"For I am persuaded, that neither death, nor life, nor angels, nor principalities, nor powers, nor things present, nor things to come, nor height, nor depth, nor any other creature shall be able to separate us from the love of God, which is in Christ Jesus."

That the Confessional Church work might be carried on, a pew-by-pew collection was taken for the purpose (the church being State supported), which proved to be the largest received since German inflation days thirteen years earlier, equalling 2,400 marks.

The following day Professor Bachnin was held by the police for distributing the petition for signatures. When the original copy was sought it seemed to have disappeared somewhere between the church and the Minister of Justice.

The same day the congregation, as well as the public, learned for the first time that on Niemoeller's being arrested the Gestapo had searched the parsonage for seven hours—tearing into mattresses; digging into nooks and corners of the furniture; taking the place apart generally in quest of incriminating evidence, hidden lists of Confessional leaders and such items. But Martin's work had been done so secretively and his tracks buried so deeply that they found no evidence to be used against him.

The following Sunday Dibelius told the people that their pastor was in good health and excellent spirits, and until then had no complaints as to the treatment he had received. He had made an appeal to the government for peace, if possible, in the religious field. It was rumored that the entire Evangelical Church with all its various sects and factions would stand solidly behind the imprisoned pastor and the Confessional Church in their endeavors to secure religious freedom in the nation.

Dibelius stood in a precarious position when he stated publicly: "Pastor Niemoeller's arrest means that the entire Christian Church of Germany has been challenged to come before the courts ... Is the Gospel of Christ to be preached in Germany, or are we to hear nothing but a German Christ from our pulpits?"

As the pastor was looking forward to a hasty trial, at least hoping for one, the Nazis ruled that it was to be conducted with utmost secrecy. When this became known on Saturday, July 13, the Confessional pastors declared that it should not be a secret matter, avowing that they would toll the bells of their churches when he went to court, calling the people for special prayer sessions at the time. The day of Niemoeller's arrest his Dahlem congregation vowed they would pray in the parish house each evening until their pastor was returned to them.

More pastor arrests began to mark the order of the day. Niemoeller's twenty-eight-year-old assistant pastor, Hildebrant, preacher at St. Anne's, was arrested on the eighteenth, and on the following Sunday Martin's brother, Wilhelm, pastor at Bielefeld, was arrested after preaching twice during the day at St. Anne's to a double congregation, and once at the Church of Jesus Christ. Crowds jammed both buildings, for they came to catch what morsels of news they might about their pastor.

Reading the list of imprisoned pastors, as Martin had taught the Confessional Church, when Wilhelm came to his brother's name he read it quietly, with a gasp from the congregation, and then prayed for all the list, but especially for his brother's release. Asking the congregation to pray for the forthcoming Oxford Church Conference soon to convene, to which Martin was to have been a delegate, he informed the people that no date had as yet been set for the church elections.

This was a victory that Martin, though in prison, had won. Wilhelm's imprisonment was of but one day's duration, and he was promptly released by the police.

On July 28 Hitler's "stooges" announced that Niemoeller was indicted on four counts: seditious activity; abuse of the pulpit; inciting disobedience to the State's decrees; and actions contrary to the minister's ordinance. It was stated that his trial was to take place not in the ordinary People's Tribunal, or criminal court, but before the Emergency Court, from whose decision there was no appeal. The following week the trial date was announced as being calendared for August 10, 12 and 16.

However, a demonstration, the like of which had not been seen since 1919, was to reset the date. On the seventh, after the usual Sunday evening service, the congregation wished to hold their customary prayer meeting for the pastor's release, but on learning that such a meeting was henceforth forbidden by the Gestapo, they decided to form a parade. Hundreds of the members gathered in the street before the Church of Jesus Christ, and marched in a near-riot demonstration.

It was the first time since the riot days of the first year after the World War that so elite a crowd behaved in such a manner. Dahlem it must be remembered is an aristocratic residential section of Berlin, the seat of the Kaiser Wilhelm Research Institute, and no other place can be found holding an equal number of trained persons, such as important business men, prosperous lawyers, professors and research scientists.

These people with their wives and young folk made up the parade, which when it started so stunned the Gestapo, who were present to enforce the no-prayer-meeting-ban, that they did not know what to think, nor what to do. Additional police were called for and a hundred and fifteen of the paraders, people of more than local consequence, were arrested.

Two days later, so great was the commotion set astir by the incident that Niemoeller's trial was indefinitely postponed.

On October 6 the trial was erased entirely from the court calendar, which was due largely to the fact that Dibelius, who had been arrested, had won a dramatic victory over Reich Church Minister Kerrl. The government did not wish to lose the court trial of Niemoeller; hence they removed it from the agenda of justice.

This day's heart-rending news for the parson was to be matched by a gladsome note when he was informed that on it his latest son had been born.

The nation was taking account of the Nazis' sour treatment of their beloved preacher. Looking into the case, the Appeals Court of Potsdam affirmed that there was no reason to hold him in prison on ordinary grounds, and had the writ of habeas corpus not been abolished in 1933, Niemoeller might have been released at the time. The court pointed out the fact that as the father of a large family he was needed to care for them, and that he had acted solely according to his conscience's dictates.

Hitler had taught the Gestapo to hold prisoners, whom they arrested without even the formality of charges being lodged against them, for an indefinite length of time. Hence there was no hope for his immediate release. This did not fit into the scheme of things, as Hitler was directing their course.

This man of iron will Adolph decided must be broken, and from past experience he knew there was no better place for this havoc to be wrought than amid the squalor and horrors of a concentration camp.

Shortly the army chaplains stepped to Martin's aid, and presented to the court a hundred-and-twenty-page defense by which they sought his release. They reported to Hitler directly that the Nazi inhumane treatment of the prisoner was affecting the army morale, which had literally divided the army, as well as the nation, into two opposing factions: the Hitler party, and the combined Confessional Church and Catholic Church.

But the dictator steeled himself to this appeal and nothing came of it. To counter these moves on the part of his friend, Hitler offered Niemoeller freedom, provided he would give his word of solemn promise not to carry on the agitation against his church regime. This way of unlocking Martin's cell doors was not new to the pastor, and he looked upon it with disdain. However, his Dahlem church received word that his health was breaking and he had suffered a number of fainting spells, making freedom the more welcome.

He coupled his refusal of Hitler's offer, given in return for licking the fuehrer's religious boots, with an application for trial or unconditional release. In his moral backbone there was not the smallest vertebra which could bend with compromise.

The following month, ninety-nine well-known pastors called personally on Hitler to halt Rosenberg's campaign as the Nazi cultural leader against the church, and to permit the churchmen to answer his derogatory insinuations and claims against the very foundation of Christianity. Hitler's answer to this was a renewed effort by the Gestapo to put more pastors in chains. During the previous eight months more than five hundred Protestant preachers had been thrown into jails. And now these were to be joined by scores and hundreds more of their brethren.

The Minister of Justice, Dr. Guertner, realizing the unnecessary and unfair treatment which Niemoeller was receiving at the hands of the police, appealed to the fuehrer to set the pastor free, but he also was refused. With the trial postponed indefinitely, Hitler dangled the promise of freedom before his prisoner, provided he would agree to drop his fight with the dictator and goosestep with the German Christians.

When Kerrl spoke on November 23, lifting his voice against the Confessional group, the persecuted pastors took this as evidence that they must set up an independent church, which their imprisoned leader had indicated as the only way to treat the current religious dictatorship. Niemoeller might be in prison, but the work which he helped bring into existence against most terrific odds was carrying on!

Chapter X

TRIAL AND CONCENTRATION CAMP

THE farce of no trial must come to an end sooner or later, and after a weary stretch of seven months, Hitler saw popular sentiment reaching such an amazing height that he determined to break this feeling by running his arch religious enemy through the hoax of a "kangaroo court" action. It was rumored that had the judges found the militant pastor not guilty they would have lost their heads no less than their benches.

During Martin's imprisonment he was busy making full preparation for his trial. When he entered the court room he wanted a brief such as no lawyer had carried upon facing a judge. He had access during the first seven months of his languishing in jail to legal volumes as well as those which discussed church jurisprudence and religious legality. He did not want to overlook a single item in the history of German ecclesiastical law that might free him.

Saturday February 6 the public was notified that Niemoeller's trial court would convene on Monday, and that for the previous seven months the State's attorneys had been busy preparing their case against him. He was accused on four counts, the same as in his original indictment. The newspapermen were told that all onlookers, including themselves, would be excluded from the court room. When the judges sat on Monday, the prisoner at the bar and a hundred and fifty Confessional preachers were admitted by card as witnesses.

147

Niemoeller marched in, lean and nervous, as he was escorted by officers and the three lawyers who were to appear for him. He brought twelve thick volumes of notes and defense arguments which he had prepared. Hitler's orders to the press were that not a word was to appear in the papers about the trial—not even indirect reference to it.

All the hatred which Niemoeller's opposition had built up in the Nazis was rampant and the atmosphere was charged with national dynamite. The eyes of the Fatherland were upon this preacher who in his pulpit had boldly defied Hitler and the combined efforts of the Gestapo.

Preliminaries over, Martin was quickly on his feet, to present his case. The State's attorney arose and wanted to know why he did not let the lawyers speak for him. Retorted the preacher, "I know more about church affairs than the attorneys." The three judges presiding admitted a motion to clear the court, and all but a few clergymen left.

A British bishop was present, but the court said it was a German trial; so he was excluded. In the corridors of the Criminal court building across the street from the United States Consulate several hundred foreigners milled about, to mingle with the groups from many Confessional parishes. While Martin was in good health and spirits, Frau Else looked wan and worn. She shortly left the room to tell friends that the pastor was well and confident in the Lord.

Clashing with the State's attorney, he asked, "Why am I here under the accusation of a traitor? I have done nothing to justify the charge." Replied the attorney, "You will find out later."

The Spring session of the Church of England Assembly opened that day and the presiding bishop said, "Let us remember in silent prayer the trial of Dr. Niemoeller."

On the first day of the trial forty-two persons testified. Throughout the sessions Niemoeller and his defendants presented evidence that the charges against him were erroneous, and should be dismissed. The judges, however, were not free to follow their own dictates in the matter.

When the evidence was weighed, Martin stood to receive sentence on three charges, but in reality was exonorated by the court as far as was possible. He was sentenced to seven months of honorable fortress imprisonment for misuse of his pulpit, but this sentence ran concurrently with the eight months he had spent in prison. Thus he had already paid the penalty demanded by the evidence presented.

He was also fined 500 marks for reading the names of parishioners who had left his church, but this was not collected in view of his long imprisonment. He did pay, however, a fine of 1,500 marks for issuing literature and signed documents, in which he urged disobedience to certain ordinances of the Church ministry. To this, court costs were added. The farce was over, but the Gestapo had another "ace up their sleeves."

Many of his followers waited at the court to see him when released. A large automobile filled with Gestapo agents forced its way through the crowd to where Pastor Niemoeller was standing. Said a secret police, "We have come to give you protection. See this crowd."

"These are my friends and I need no protection," replied the preacher.

"The Gestapo is taking you into protective custody," came the answer. And he was forced into the car, to be driven away immediately. He was a free man at last, news of which large groups of his members awaited at the Dahlem church. But the news they received was of a different nature as an assistant pastor told them that Niemoeller upon being released was immediately arrested by the Gestapo, and placed in the Alexanderplatz Prison.

The fact that Martin had been free for a short time was as tragic a blow to Kerrl as his rearrest was to his friends. When the Gestapo took him in hand the second time his wife collapsed, for she and his children never expected to see him again. After being celled in the Moabit prison for so many months, he was taken at once to the Sachsenhausen concentration camp, which is not a great distance from Berlin. Here the iron heel of Gestapo cruelty, as Adolph thought, would crush the spirit out of Martin.

But that March 2, when he was rearrested, was to be marked with as fine a martyr spirit as the ages have ever witnessed. Martin knew not the fate which tomorrow would fling across his path. He expected it to be the worst physical, mental and spiritual fare with which the Nazis could gorge a prisoner. But his eyes were beyond the stars and his hope was Heaven-high. Though expecting death, he could be joyously enwrapped in the knowledge that a mansion awaited him at the gates of death— a Heaven which he had found proclaimed in the Bible, for which he was willing to give his life, and which he nobly preached to others.

His first letter from the concentration camp gloriously announced to Hitler and the world that his faith was grounded on the Rock of salvation. "How fine not to have to learn anew that the Rock remains unshakable in whatever may befall us," he wrote.

In July of 1938 it was again rumored that Hitler had offered this martyr-minded man his freedom, provided he would fall down and worship at the German Christian shrine over which the Nazi leader presided as lord of Germany and self-styled ruler of the universe.

On the ninth of the following January, 1939, Wilhelm Niemoeller, Martin's preacher brother, said at the Dahlem church, "A sham synod is now being created to merge all elements within the church under the State compulsion. The church has its authority from God and cannot approve such a development and the German people who walk in darkness are beginning to see a great light."

Thus the struggle was being carried on by the *Bekenntniskirche,* the Confessional Church, and there was no waning in the struggle, even though their leader was under Hitler's iron rule. When Confessional pastors read the names of those in prison, including Niemoeller's, the congregations stood for the fifteen or twenty minutes which this required. The reading was followed by prayer to sustain those who were willing to die for their faith.

Kerrl passed three regulatory devices by which he aimed to break the Confessional Church, and which he hoped, with Niemoeller out of the way, would destroy all traces of the religious battle. The first method used was to offer a better church to a Confessional preacher who was causing difficulty—one in which the elements of the German Christian group were strong. This move was merely to lead up to the second and more dangerous ruse. A church minority was empowered to make application for a new pastor when they did not like the present one. Thus even a handful of German Christians were able to oust a Confessional preacher.

The third decree endowed the Church Council with autonomous powers by which it was supreme, and its actions in no wise were touchable by synods or local churches, or amenable to any but Hitler. Thus a pastor could be changed at will by this Council, and the local congregation's voice was stilled in any appeal.

During the year Dr. Ewart Edmund Turner, former minister of the American Church in Berlin and friend of Niemoeller, said, "Niemoeller's physical and mental health is noticeably suffering." He had battled a severe attack of intestinal influenza whose ravages nearly approached the terrors of pneumonia in a concentration camp.

Martin lost the grip upon his emotions at this time, and decided it was best for him not to partake of the communion sacrament. This was a blow; for as a churchman he was most strict, and to him the sacrament of the Lord's Supper brought a close spiritual contact with the Lord, of whose body he partook in the emblems.

There was a bright hope for him each month, and this was his fifteen-mile trip to Berlin for a brief visit with his wife and one child. Later he was permitted only to see his wife, for the strain on the children proved too much for them.

In the cell at the camp there was only a scrawny bed, a bare table and a chair, immersed in a death-like silence. He was permitted the use of his Bible, though later even the New Testament was taken from him; but he was not allowed to write more than a few brief notes on the Scriptures. For it was re-membered by the Gestapo that Hitler's imprisonment proved the seed ground from which his program for world dominance sprouted. The Nazis are fearful that if Martin were given the guns of authorship, he would fire a wordy barrage that would be the un-doing of them.

The windows of his cell for many weary months were boarded almost to the ceiling, and the only view Niemoeller had of the outside world was the blue sky and the heavens above—especially the heavens above.

Twice a month he was allowed the luxury of writing his wife, which letters were domineeringly censored. In one of these he simply scrawled, "II Cor. 4:16"—which reads "For which cause we faint not; but though our outward man perish, yet the in-ward man is renewed day by day." In that tiny cell he reread the Bible three times, and was blessed with the privilege of memorizing three hundred hymns, whose reservoir of spiritual strength he daily tapped.

While thus in the Sachsenhausen concentration camp, Dr. Frederick Werner of the Evangelical Church endeavored to oust Martin from his Dahlem pastorate. Though imprisoned he held the post, and if this were taken from him it meant that his family would be cut off without financial assistance.

The faithful congregation arose to a man in this hour of the Niemoeller need, and said, "You, Mr. President, have attempted through arbitrary measures that disregard all legal principles of the church, to vest in yourself a number of powers and rights that are in themselves devoid of legality. You are attempting now to burden further our sorely tried Pastor Niemoeller with worry for the welfare of his wife and seven children. This is not a Christian action and in so doing you are only forcing the Confessional Church into a new defensive position.

"The Dahlem community successfully defended itself against attempts by Reichsbishop Ludwig Muller to force on them a new minister in place of Pastor Niemoeller. The Dahlem community is determined to defend itself again. We consider Pastor Niemoeller, though he may be imprisoned, as our rightfully chosen minister and we hold thereto in all faith."

This closed the matter and let Hitler know that however he might try he was unable to break the backbone of the Confessional Church, of which the Dahlem parish was the leading light.

As the second anniversary of his imprisonment approached, July 1, 1939, Martin now broken in health drew up his last will and testament, in which he gave instruction to Frau Else as to his burial.

The Nazis, thinking at the time of his arrest that the matter would soon be over, and that Martin would be forgotten, had issued through Chantre, the Gestapo leader, a statement saying, "A trifling pulpit announcement from a handful of Confessional pastors, and then after a few days the case is forgotten." Chantre was assigned to take charge of the Berlin

drive against Martin's brethren in the faith. But
after two years he found the group a stronger and
more formidable enemy than ever.

When the war was looming large on the horizon
of German life, Martin told his wife that he was
ready to enter submarine warfare once again. On
September 24, he volunteered for U-boat service,
which was speedily declined by Hitler. At the time
he was still in the camp on Berlin's outskirts, where
the only papers he saw were those which advocated
Nazi policy and were Gestapo-censored. What he
knew of world conditions came to him through the
haze of Nazi dominance, and was colored as Hitler
desired. As a full-hearted German, he loved his
Fatherland, and in war as well as in peace he was
ready to die for her.

He was now willing to take his place in a submarine—one of the subs that had sent enemy ships
to burial in the sea's depths—and ply the waters for
his country. But even this service Hitler would not
permit him to render. He had set out to break
Niemoeller body and soul, and the dictator was not
willing to risk freeing Martin's mind from the
terrors of the concentration camp even at the price
of sinking hostile ships.

Early in 1940 Father and Mother Niemoeller were
celebrating their golden wedding anniversary.
Supremely above all else they wished their son to be
present to take part in the ceremony and to complete
the family circle. That this might be made possible,
eight hundred naval officers and a similar number of
prominent laymen in the Reich offered themselves
as hostages that he might be temporarily released
from the camp.

For not one moment did Hitler consider releasing the man who had brought him more trouble of conscience and more defiance than any other in the Reich. The answer sent to those leading citizens and officers was negative. In prison he was, and there he must remain. At the time he was in solitary confinement and there were rumors in Scandinavia that his health was rapidly failing.

It was a joyous occasion for the grand old pair of lovers, and Martin, though absent, made up a part of the celebrating circle. They had gathered at Bielefeld for the jubilation of fifty years of wedded bliss. All the Niemoellers were there except two: Martin in the concentration camp, and a son of Wilhelm, a Confessional pastor, who was studying in England.

For the first time Martin was permitted to write his parents from Sachsenhausen, and the letter brought pleasure to Heinrich and Paula. To them it was one of their most beloved possessions. Martin said, "Include me in the celebrants of your golden wedding anniversary, not as a sad guest but as the merriest of all, and the helper of your joy."

Had he been able to attend the anniversary of his aged parents it would have remained a bright spot in Martin's memory throughout his life. For on March 23, 1941, Heinrich laid down his battle weapons, folded his hands, left to the design of God the fate of his fighting son, and answered his eternal call.

When Niemoeller offered his services for submarine activity the second time, and was refused, it attracted considerable attention throughout the Christian world, most of which was then suffering untold damages and spiritual demolition from Hitler's armies.

Karl Barth, famed Swiss theologian, writing in *La Semaine Religieuse* of Geneva, came forward with a plausible explanation in the Confessional leader's behalf.

"Niemoeller did offer his services," he said, "to the German navy, and then he withdrew the offer. Later on he made it again. He then received a negative reply in a rather nasty spirit . . . Do not forget that Niemoeller is also a good, a too-good Lutheran. Lutheranism permits and demands the belief that there is a real chasm between the essential and the political . . . He is capable of permitting himself to be put to death by Hitler in the cause of Christ, but he is also capable of being an officer on a warship of that same Hitler."

According to the newspaper *Het Volk* when Martin offered his services the second time, Grand Admiral Erich Raeder rasped out the official "No."

Barth in a letter also said, "We must not forget that Niemoeller was always a good, a very good German, and he has so remained to this day. He fought valiantly in the war of 1914-18, convinced as he was of the justice of the German cause. Later he became a pastor, a very good pastor. But his old Adam—as with all of us—is not dead.

"I do not believe he lost his head when he offered his services to Hitler, but I believe he simply acted in the spirit which his old Adam—or human nature —dictated."

On February 4, 1941, the world was astounded by the words which Louis P. Lochner, head of the Associated Press of Germany, wirelessed, saying,

"Protestant circles received reports today that Reverend Martin Niemoeller has become converted to Catholicism." The wire carried a note that for some time the pastor had been studying Catholic writings in his cell at the Sachsenhausen concentration camp. This was followed by a wire that his wife and Dahlem friends were greatly disturbed by the news.

Six days later Frau Else visited with her husband, and on returning to Dahlem she denied flatly that he had changed his church allegiance. How the rumor flashed into being that he had sent a petition to the Berlin Catholic Bishopric for admission is not known. But this is true: had Martin made the change, he recognized that it would not in the least alter his status before Hitler. For in the same concentration camp there are many Catholic priests and nuns, all of whom are as vilely treated as the pastor.

It is known that Martin studied Catholic doctrine for more than three years, hoping to bring about a closer collaboration between the Confessional Church and the Catholics in their common fight against Hitler's usurpation of all religious authority. He had also sent for the Book of Common Prayer, which he studied, wishing to learn more about Evangelical catholicism, or the church universal.

Martin closed the pro and con argument of his religious church membership when on March 10, 1941, Confessional pastors read to their congregations his own denial of an intention to become a Catholic. He asked his friends to refute all such rumors, whatever their source or dominant interest.

The common belief is by those who understand Hitler's propaganda psychology that the Gestapo or other high Nazi sources fostered the rumor and gave it the greatest publicity, hoping thereby to throw confusion into the Confessional Church. They thought that such a move would weaken the defiant pastors who yet remained outside concentration camps. The result, however, was just the opposite, and really strengthened the resistance of Martin's followers against Hitler's German Christians.

Two weeks after Niemoeller's denial he was shocked by the death of his father, upon whose shoulders had recently rested a part of the Confessional burden he himself had borne when free.

The latest authentic word received as to Niemoeller's activities came on August 29, 1941, when it was reported that he was transferred to a Bavarian concentration camp at Dachau. The move greatly improved his health. Here he shares a three-room cell with two Catholic priests and holds conversations and engages in lively theological discussions with his cellmates. The pastor read to them the works of Fritz Reuter, the outstanding Low-German poet-novelist.

His wife still makes her monthly visit to see him, but beyond this, little is known about his present activities. The Confessional Church, stiffening its resistance to Hitler's religious demands, is growing, because its members are holding aloft the Christian banner of true religion as Martin taught them before his imprisonment.

If he is never permitted to preach again—if before the firing squad he meets his death—or lays his head on the block before Hitler's sharp ax—he has the knowledge that recently his three sons sent him these glorious words: "We will follow in your steps and become ministers."

Recently the pastor's three oldest sons went to their mother, so word came through the German underground movement, and reaffirmed their desire to be ministers, saying, "Mother, the three of us have decided to go into the Christian ministry, we admire Father so much." Her eyes shone with a new luster as she told of this incident.

In February, 1943, it was rumored Niemoeller had been released from prison with the hope that when the inevitable Nazi crash came through an Allied victory the pastor would be able to assume a national leadership and soften the peace terms. This rumor, however, has not been verified. On July 1, 1943, he began his seventh year in a concentration camp. To the best of available information at this writing (August 10, 1943), he is still at Dachau, which recent reports indicate has become something of a specialized camp for religious prisoners. His health continues, according to these reports, to be good.

During the past seven years, true to their promise, from fifty to a hundred members and friends have gathered each night at Niemoeller's Berlin church to pray for their pastor. Recent bombings have not changed these seven-year-old prayer meetings. These people believe God is still on the throne and is stronger than Hitler or any Nazi combinations of evil, and well able to *deliver!*

Thus whatever fate may befall him—whether he steps out of the concentration camp alive, or feels Hitler's sharp ax on his neck,—he is willing to live for Christ, whom he preached so grandly, or die for Him, who gave His life that Martin Niemoeller, U-boat captain, dynamic preacher, concentration camp prisoner, might live.

"The earthly pillars of our hope are falling away," he said a few months before imprisonment. "The prospects of better times are leaving us in the lurch ... But the Lord Jesus Christ lives, and He is present. He asks us to believe, to sacrifice. May God help us to say with Paul, 'For me to live is Christ!' Then we shall see the glory of God."

This faith sustains him with an unfaltering trust, faith in a living, ever-present Redeemer. Hitler may break his body, but never his soul! Hitler may lift the swastika high over Germany, but never high enough to blot out Niemoeller's vision of the Cross! Hitler may rule the fatherland as fuehrer, but Martin's cry is, "God is my Fuehrer."

Printed in the United States of America